STUDY GUIDE TO ACCOMPANY

FAMILY LAW
THE ESSENTIALS

WILLIAM P. STATSKY

PREPARED BY
BRENDA L. RICE
Johnson County Community College
Overland Park, Kansas

WEST PUBLISHING COMPANY
MINNEAPOLIS/ST. PAUL   NEW YORK   LOS ANGELES   SAN FRANCISCO

Cover image: *Lofting Model,* bronze, 1991. Sculptor: Paul T. Granlund. Represented by Premier Gallery, Minneapolis. Sculpture photography: Stan Waldhauser.

WEST'S COMMITMENT TO THE ENVIRONMENT

In 1906, West Publishing Company began recycling materials left over from the production of books. This began a tradition of efficient and responsible use of resources. Today, 100% of our legal bound volumes are printed on acid-free, recycled paper consisting of 50% new fibers. West recycles nearly 27,700,000 pounds of scrap paper annually—the equivalent of 229,300 trees. Since the 1960s, West has devised ways to capture and recycle waste inks, solvents, oils, and vapors created in the printing process. We also recycle plastics of all kinds, wood, glass, corrugated cardboard, and batteries, and have eliminated the use of polystyrene book packaging. We at West are proud of the longevity and the scope of our commitment to the environment.

West pocket parts and advance sheets are printed on recyclable paper and can be collected and recycled with newspapers. Staples do not have to be removed. Bound volumes can be recycled after removing the cover.

Production, Prepress, Printing and Binding by West Publishing Company.

TEXT IS PRINTED ON 10% POST CONSUMER RECYCLED PAPER

COPYRIGHT © 1997 by WEST PUBLISHING CO.
　　　　　　　　　　　　610 Opperman Drive
　　　　　　　　　　　　P.O. Box 64526
　　　　　　　　　　　　St. Paul, MN 55164–0526

All rights reserved
Printed in the United States of America
04 03 02 01 00 99   8 7 6 5 4 3 2

ISBN 0–314–20838–0

CONTENTS

Chapter 1. THE SCOPE OF A FAMILY LAW PRACTICE
        Review of Chapter   1
        Review Questions   1
        Practice Exercises   3
        Answers to Review Questions   5

Chapter 2. BREACH OF PROMISE TO MARRY, THE HEART-BALM STATUTE, AND CONTRACTS RESTRAINING MARRIAGE
        Review of Chapter   6
        Review Questions   6
        Practice Exercises   11
        Answers to Review Questions   12

Chapter 3. ANTENUPTIAL AGREEMENTS AND COHABITATION AGREEMENTS
        Review of Chapter   14
        Review Questions   14
        Practice Exercises   19
        Answers to Review Questions   20

Chapter 4. THE FORMATION OF CEREMONIAL MARRIAGES AND COMMON LAW MARRIAGES
        Review of Chapter   22
        Review Questions   22
        Practice Exercises   26
        Answers to Review Questions   28

Chapter 5. ANNULMENT
        Review of Chapter   30
        Review Questions   30
        Practice Exercises   35
        Answers to Review Questions   36

Chapter 6. SEPARATION AGREEMENTS: LEGAL ISSUES AND DRAFTING OPTIONS
        Review of Chapter   38

Review Questions	38
Practice Exercises	42
Answers to Review Questions	44

Chapter 7. CHILD CUSTODY

Review of Chapter	46
Review Questions	46
Practice Exercises	51
Answers to Review Questions	53

Chapter 8. CHILD SUPPORT

Review of Chapter	55
Review Questions	55
Practice Exercises	60
Answers to Review Questions	62

Chapter 9. DIVORCE, JUDICIAL SEPARATION, AND SEPARATE MAINTENANCE

Review of Chapter	64
Review Questions	64
Practice Exercises	68
Answers to Review Questions	70

Chapter 10. DIVORCE PROCEDURE

Review of Chapter	72
Review Questions	72
Practice Exercises	77
Answers to Review Questions	78

Chapter 11. TAX CONSEQUENCES OF SEPARATION AND DIVORCE

Review of Chapter	80
Review Questions	80
Practice Exercises	84
Answers to Review Questions	86

Chapter 12. THE LEGAL RIGHTS OF WOMEN

Review of Chapter	88
Review Questions	88
Practice Exercises	93
Answers to Review Questions	94

Chapter 13. ILLEGITIMACY AND PATERNITY PROCEEDINGS

Review of Chapter	96

Review Questions	96
Practice Exercises	101
Answers to Review Questions	102

Chapter 14. THE LEGAL STATUS OF CHILDREN

Review of Chapter	104
Review Questions	104
Practice Exercises	108
Answers to Review Questions	109

Chapter 15. ADOPTION

Review of Chapter	111
Review Questions	111
Practice Exercises	116
Answers to Review Questions	117

Chapter 16. SURROGACY AND THE NEW SCIENCE OF MOTHERHOOD

Review of Chapter	119
Review Questions	119
Practice Exercises	123
Answers to Review Questions	124

Chapter 17. TORTS

Review of Chapter	126
Review Questions	126
Practice Exercises	131
Answers to Review Questions	132

Chapter 1

THE SCOPE OF A FAMILY LAW PRACTICE

REVIEW OF CHAPTER:

Family law typically includes divorce, custody, and support. Occasionally family law problems also involve criminal law, contract law, property law, tort law, civil procedure, evidence, juvenile law, tax law, and estate law. The role of a family law paralegal depends on the supervising attorney, but often family law paralegals conduct interviews, draft pleadings, gather information, and prepare discovery requests.

REVIEW QUESTIONS:

Multiple choice.
Select the correct answer from the choices provided.

1. Often family law problems require knowledge of other legal areas such as:

    a. criminal law
    b. property law
    c. tort law
    d. estate law
    e. all of the above

2. Paralegal responsibilities in a family law practice may include:

    a. conducting initial interviews
    b. performing field investigations
    c. conducting legal research
    d. a and c only
    e. all of the above

3. If a family law paralegal is engaged in "discovery", the paralegal may be:

    a. conducting an initial client interview

b. preparing documents for transfer of assets
   (c.) preparing answers to interrogatories
   d. drafting stipulations for temporary orders
   e. all of the above

4. If a family law paralegal is performing a task related to a hearing, the paralegal may be:

   a. assisting in preparation of exhibits
   b. preparing witnesses and clients
   c. developing forms for gathering client information
   d. all of the above
   (e.) a and b, only

5. If a family law paralegal is performing a "post decree" related task, the paralegal may be:

   a. drafting a separation agreement
   (b.) preparing documents for transfer of assets
   c. arranging for service of process
   d. preparing discovery requests
   e. all of the above

Fill in the blank.
Fill in the blank with a term from Chapter 1.

1. When gathering information in a divorce matter, it will be important for the paralegal to determine how __title__ to real or personal property is held.

2. In a divorce matter which involves ownership of a business, it will be important for the paralegal to determine whether the business is a corporation, a sole proprietorship, or a __partnership__.

3. An issue of civil procedure which may arise in a divorce matter is which court has __jurisdiction__ to hear the case.

4. A primary purpose of the initial client interview is to obtain information which will be used by the paralegal in drafting initial __pleadings__, such as the petition.

5. The field of law which may be relevant to particular issues involving children is known as ___juvenile___ law.

Short Answer.
Answer each of the following questions in one or two sentences.

1. Explain how tax law could be relevant to a divorce case.

2. Identify a particular situation in which the rules of ethics would affect a paralegal's communication with the opposing side in a divorce matter.

3. Why is "discovery" considered to play ana important role in family law?

PRACTICE EXERCISES:

1. Locate a "form book" in your law library which contains some sample pleadings which could be used to draft documents which would be filed in a divorce action in your state.
a) Identify the paragraphs in your form which contain statements or concepts which relate to the financial aspects of the divorce.
b) Identify the paragraphs in your which contain statements or concepts which relate to the child custody aspects of the divorce.

2. Use a legal thesaurus to identify synonyms for the following terms:
a) divorce
b) child custody
c) complaint
d) marriage
e) support

3. Assume that you have been asked to draft an initial complain for divorce to be filed on behalf of your firm's client. Before you begin, you should identify any statutory or case law which may be relevant. Prepare a list of words which would be useful to you to

search the indexes of codes and digests relevant to your state.

4. Using your list of words (created in question 3, above), search the index of your state statutes and make a list of the statutes (by their numbers) which relate to divorce proceedings.

ANSWERS TO REVIEW QUESTIONS:

Multiple choice.

1. E
2. E
3. C
4. E
5. B

Fill in the blank.

1. title
2. partnership
3. jurisdiction
4. pleadings
5. juvenile

Short answer.

1. Tax law may impact on the property settlement. There may be a refund due or the parties may not have filed tax returns. Tax law will be important in negotiating matters of child custody and support.

2. If an opposing party is represented by an attorney, the paralegal must communicate only with the attorney, not directly with the opposing party.

3. "Discovery" is an important part of family law because it is the method by which information is gathered concerning assets, liabilities, and other relevant matters which will affect the outcome of property distribution, custody, and support.

Chapter 2

BREACH OF PROMISE TO MARRY, THE HEART-BALM STATUTE, AND CONTRACTS RESTRAINING MARRIAGE

REVIEW OF CHAPTER:

Heartbalm actions are legal actions filed for breaking a promise to marry. Many states have enacted heartbalm statutes which abolish this contract action. In some states, actions may be filed as torts for fraud or for intentional infliction of emotional distress. The elements of the contract action are offer, acceptance, consideration, capacity, and compliance with the statute of frauds, if applicable. Fraud requires the plaintiff to prove the defendant knowingly made a false statement of present fact with intention that plaintiff rely on the statement, reasonable reliance, and damages. Intentional infliction of emotional distress requires the plaintiff to show the defendant intentionally caused severe emotional distress by extreme or outrageous conduct. Monetary damages which may be awarded in these cases could include compensatory damages for actual expenses, aggravated damages for special circumstances, and punitive damages awarded to punish the defendant for particularly malicious or deceitful conduct.

Problems may arise when gifts are given to the prospective bride or groom and the engagement is later broken. A gift is irrevocable if there was voluntary delivery, intent to relinquish title and control, no consideration or conditions, and acceptance. When gifts are given on the condition that the wedding take place, they are not irrevocable, and a court may require that they be returned to the donor.

Contracts which involve a general restraint on marriage are unenforceable. Courts may enforce agreements which are found to be reasonable, partial, or useful restraints on marriage.

REVIEW QUESTIONS:

Multiple choice.
Select the correct answer from the choices provided.

1. Heart balm actions (where recognized) may be filed under which of these legal theories?

    a. breach of contract

b. negligence
c. wrongful termination
d. fraud
e. a and d

2. A remedy which courts will NOT award in heart balm actions is:

   a. punitive damages
   b. specific performance
   c. compensatory damages
   d. monetary damages
   e. exemplary damages

3. Some states which have abolished breach of promise to marry actions have done so by enacting legislation known as:

   a. heart balm statutes
   b. heart balm actions
   c. mitigation of damages
   d. statutes of limitations
   e. statutes of frauds

4. Compensatory damages which may be awarded in a heart balm action could include:

   a. plaintiff's actual out-of-pocket expenses
   b. plaintiff's lost income
   c. cost of purchasing a wedding gown
   d. all of the above
   e. none of the above

5. In some cases, mitigating circumstances will justify a reduction in damages awarded to the plaintiff. An example of mitigating circumstance is:

   a. plaintiff was very wealthy
   b. plaintiff was pregnant
   c. plaintiff never loved defendant
   d. defendant broke the engagement
   e. defendant acted maliciously

6. In order for a gift to be irrevocable, the donor must intend:

a. that the gift is conditional on the marriage
b. to actually deliver the gift at a later date
c. that the gift be effective immediately
d. that the donee pay for the gift
e. that the donee accept the gift

7. An example of a gift which is conditional would be:

a. a birthday present
b. a wedding present
c. an expensive ring
d. an anniversary present
e. none of the above

8. An example of an unlawful contract restraining marriage is:

a. Marilyn's father forbids her to marry Richard
b. Richard's father agrees to pay for Richard's college education if Richard agrees not to marry Marilyn until he graduates
c. Marilyn's mother agrees to pay for Marilyn and Richard's honeymoon trip if they agree to get married in a church
d. Richard's mother's will leaves Richard $50,000 if Richard promises not to marry

9. If defendant in a heart balm action has intentionally deceived plaintiff and acted maliciously in an effort to cause plaintiff extreme humiliation and emotional suffering, plaintiff may be able to recover _____ damages in addition to money for actual expenses incurred.

a. punitive
b. monetary
c. compensatory
d. equitable
e. mitigated

10. The requirement that certain contracts be in writing in order to be enforceable is the:

a. statute of limitations
b. heart balm statute
c. cause of action
d. mitigation
e. statute of frauds

Fill in the blank.
Fill in the blank with a term from Chapter 2.

1. An agreement that a court will enforce is a __CONTRACT__

2. An allegation of facts that gives a party a right to receive relief from a court is a __CAUSE OF ACTION__.

3. Money awarded by a court to make the injured party whole or restore the injured party to the position he or she was in before the injury or loss is known as __compensatory__ damages.

4. Money awarded by a court to cover special circumstances that justify an increase in the amount awarded as actual damages is known as __aggravated damages__

5. In contracts, __consideration__ is something of value that is exchanged between the parties as a basis of the bargain.

6. Parties to a contract must have __capasity__, the legal power to enter into a binding agreement.

7. In an action for breach of promise to marry, the element of consideration will usually be the parties' exchange of __promises__.

8. A remedy for breach of contract (not usually awarded in heart balm actions) that forces the wrongdoing party to complete the contract as promised is __specific performance__.

9. Some states have abolished actions for breach of promise to marry by enacting legislation known as __heart balm statute__.

10. Money spent by plaintiff in a heart balm action for purchases such as a wedding dress, wedding rings and invitations are __out-of-pocket__ expenses, which may be recovered as compensatory damages.

11. A tort action which could be filed against a defendant who asked plaintiff to marry, when defendant had no intention of ever marrying plaintiff is an action for __fraud__.

12. A tort action which could be filed against a defendant who asked plaintiff to marry for the sole purpose of causing plaintiff severe psychological harm is an action for __intentional infliction of emotional distress__.

13. A gift which is completely given and cannot be recalled is __irrevocable__.

14. When deciding whether to enforce a contract which restrains marriage, courts will consider whether the restraint is a __General__ restraint or a __reasonable__ limitation.

15. A gift of personal property in a will is a __bequest__.

Short answer.
Answer each of the following questions in one or two sentences.

1. Why have some states eliminated heart balm actions?

2. In states which have abolished breach of promise to marry actions, what other legal theories do plaintiffs occasionally use to bring heart balm actions?

3. Under what circumstances might a "heart balm" plaintiff be allowed to recover aggravated damages?

4. Under what circumstances could the recipient of an engagement ring be required by a court to return the ring to the donor?

5. Under what circumstances does a gift become irrevocable?

6. What public policy or purpose could be used to explain why courts do not enforce contracts restraining marriage?

7. Under what circumstances might a court reduce an award of damages to a plaintiff in a heart balm action?

8. Under what circumstances might a court make an award of punitive damages to a plaintiff in a heart balm action?

PRACTICE EXERCISES:

1. Assume that our client is the successful plaintiff in a heart balm action (in a state which allows such claims). The trial court has awarded damages for the following harm: a) wedding dress, $1200.; b) invitations, $300; c) reception, $5,000;
d) wedding rings, $3,200; e) lost income, $3,000; f) seduction and resulting pregnancy, $4,500; g) malicious humiliation by defendant, $2,000; h) injury to reputation, $1,000.

    a) Which of these items should be classified as punitive damages; b) which are compensatory damages; and c) which are aggravated damages?

2. Review the facts in the case of Bob and Mary (see Assignment 2.3 in chapter two of the text). Draft a Complaint which could be filed on behalf of Bob against Mary in which he seeks to recover the car and engagement ring.

ANSWERS TO REVIEW QUESTIONS:

Multiple choice.

1. E
2. B
3. A
4. D
5. C
6. C
7. B
8. D
9. A
10. E

Fill in the blank.

1. contract
2. cause of action
3. compensatory damages
4. aggravated damages
5. consideration
6. capacity
7. promises
8. specific performance
9. heart balm statutes
10. out-of-pocket
11. fraud
12. intentional infliction of emotional distress
13. irrevocable
14. general, reasonable
15. bequest

Short answer.

1. Courts do not favor this type of legal proceeding because it requires the plaintiff to discuss very personal and perhaps embarrassing facts. Also, it is not an unusual situation for an engaged couple to break up. States do not support a policy which would encourage someone to marry who doesn't wish to do so. Marriages today are seldom viewed as business

arrangements or as opportunities to acquire wealth.

2. fraud, intentional infliction of emotional distress

3. the defendant seduced the plaintiff, a pregnancy resulted, or plaintiff endured extreme humiliation as a result of unusual publicity

4. when the ring is a conditional gift, conditioned on the marriage occurring

5. donor intends to transfer title or possession of the gift immediately, gift is transferred to the donee, donee accepts, gift is voluntarily given, gift is unconditional, no consideration is given for the gift

6. Marriage is recognized as a positive relationship in our society. Public policy supports allowing individuals to be free to marry anyone he or she chooses. To interfere with the right to marry would violate public policy.

7. plaintiff did not love defendant, defendant broke up with true regard to plaintiff's feelings, plaintiff was marrying for money only

8. defendant deceived plaintiff intentionally, defendant acted with malice to intentionally humiliate plaintiff

Chapter 3

ANTENUPTIAL AGREEMENTS AND COHABITATION AGREEMENTS

REVIEW OF CHAPTER:

Couples who intend to marry or who intend to live together without marrying sometimes enter agreements which define certain rights and obligations to each other. An antenuptial agreement is made between two people who intend to marry. A cohabitation agreement is made between two people who intend to live together without being married.

Antenuptial agreements must meet the requirements for valid contracts, must be based on disclosure of assets, must not be unconscionable, and must not violate public policy. Most states require antenuptial agreements to be written. Terms of these agreements often affect property ownership and distribution at divorce or death.

Cohabitation agreements may be express or implied contracts. If no such contractual agreement can be proven, other theories of recovery include trust, partnership, joint venture, and the putative-spouse doctrine. Court decisions have stated differing views on the enforceability of cohabitation agreements, but generally they are enforceable as long as the contract does not violate public policy.

REVIEW QUESTIONS:

Multiple choice.
Select the correct answer from the choices provided.

1. An antenuptial agreement is also called:

    a. a cohabitation agreement
    b. a prenuptial agreement
    c. a constructive trust
    d. a postmarital agreement

2. A contract made by two individuals who intend to live together without being married is:

a. a cohabitation agreement
b. an antenuptial agreement
c. an implied contract
d. a meretricious contract
e. unenforceable

3. Antenuptial agreements may <u>not</u>:

    a. affect ownership of real property at death
    b. waive a wife's right to receive support after divorce
    c. adversely affect child support
    d. be signed prior to marriage
    e. be more favorable to one party

4. The number of couples who sign antenuptial agreements can be attributed to societal factors such as:

    a. high divorce rate
    b. couples marrying at an older age
    c. increase in number of couples living together without being married
    d. a and b
    e. b and c

5. Although states' laws vary, most states have a Statute of Frauds which requires antenuptial agreements to be:

    a. notarized
    b. witnessed by two disinterested parties
    c. drafted by an attorney
    d. signed at least three days before the marriage ceremony
    e. in writing

6. If the court finds _____ at the time an antenuptial agreement was signed, the court will invalidate the agreement.

    a. fraud
    b. duress
    c. disclosure of assets
    d. either a or b
    e. either a, b, or c

7. One of the main objectives of an antenuptial agreement is:

   a. to take away rights spouses would otherwise have in each other's assets
   b. to provide an opportunity for prospective spouses to disclose property assets to each other
   c. to reduce the rate of divorce
   d. to encourage prospective spouses to agree on the division of household chores

8. The case which is generally recognized for giving unmarried couples an opportunity to have a court resolve support and property issues upon termination of the relationship is:

   a. DeLorean v. DeLorean
   b. Marvin v. Marvin
   c. Hewitt v. Hewitt
   d. Watts v. Watts
   e. none of the above

9. Cohabitation agreements will not be valid if:

   a. the parties were never married to each other
   b. the parties cohabited
   c. an express condition of the agreement is an unlawful sexual relationship
   d. the sexual aspect of the relationship is not severable from the rest of the agreement
   e. both c and d.

10. A cohabitation agreement which is clearly discussed and intended by the parties, but which is not written is:

    a. an implied contract
    b. a quasi-contract
    c. an express contract
    d. a trust
    e. unenforceable

Fill in the blank.
Fill in the blank with a term from Chapter 3.

1. A legal entity that exists when one person holds property for the benefit of another is a ___trust___.

Chapter 3   STUDY GUIDE   17

2. A contract not created by the parties, but created by law to avoid unjust enrichment is a _____.

3. Courts require adequate _disclosure_ of assets by both parties to an antenuptial agreement.

4. A contract that will not be enforced because it is so substantially unfair is said to be _invalid_.

5. Although many states do not require any consideration for an antenuptial agreement, the _____ of the parties is recognized as valid consideration in most states.

6. A voluntary agreement between two or more persons to use their resources in a business or other venture, with the understanding that they will proportionately share losses and profits is a _partnership_.

7. An agreement to participate in a common enterprise in which the parties have a mutual right of control is a _____.

8. In some states, a person who reasonably believed that he or she was validly married when, in fact, a legal impediment made the marriage unlawful will be recognized as a _____.

9. An unlawful or illicit sexual relationship is known as a _____ relationship.

10. Courts will usually not enforce a waiver of spousal support contained in an antenuptial agreement if the result of divorce would be that the disadvantaged spouse will depend on _____ for financial resources.

11. If a party can prove that he or she did not sign the antenuptial agreement _____, a court will not enforce the agreement.

12. Principles that are generally recognized as naturally and inherently right, which when violated may require a court to invalidate an agreement, are principles based on _____.

13. Individuals who _____, whether married or not, live together and share a close relationship.

14. A clause or portion of a contract which is _____ can be removed from the

contract without destroying what remains.

15. A nonlegal term for support payments made by one party to another after a non-marital relationship ends is _____.

Short answer.
Answer each of the following questions in one or two sentences.

1. What types of terms or matters may be covered in an antenuptial agreement?

2. Identify four circumstances in which a court would find an antenuptial agreement to be unenforceable.

3. What public policy argument could be made against cohabitation agreements?

4. What public policy argument could be made in favor of cohabitation agreements?

5. Why is "palimony" an inaccurate term?

6. What is the primary difference between an express and an implied contract?

7. What characteristics are typical of couples who sign antenuptial agreements?

8. Why is disclosure of assets such a significant requirement for a court to uphold an antenuptial

agreement?

9. What is meant by a "meretricious" relationship?

10. Why has the theory that "antenuptial agreements encourage divorce and, therefore, violate public policy" become less popular?

PRACTICE EXERCISES:

1. Assume that you are preparing to enter into an antenuptial agreement. Make a list of the assets you own which should be disclosed to your prospective spouse prior to signing the agreement. Now make a list of the assets which your prospective spouse owns.

   What is the approximate value of each of your total assets? If each of you agrees to waive all rights to claim any interest in the property of the other, will this agreement be enforceable? Why or why not?

2. Under the Uniform Premarital Agreement Act antenuptial agreements may not adversely impact the rights of children to receive child support in the event their parents divorce. Draft an enforceable paragraph in which the parties to such an agreement address the payment of child support.

3. Look at your state's statutes concerning antenuptial agreements. Make a checklist of the specific requirements for a valid agreement under the laws of your state. (For example, items on your checklist might include a) must be in writing, b) must be notarized, c) must be supported by consideration.)

4. Locate a case from a court in your state in which the court granted support or property to a party whose non-marital relationship terminated. On what legal theory did the court grant relief? (ex. express contract, quasi-contract, trust) Make a list of all other legal theories of relief which were mentioned by the court. Which of these other theories could be the basis for such relief in your state?

ANSWERS TO REVIEW QUESTIONS:

Multiple choice.

1. B
2. A
3. C
4. D
5. E
6. D
7. A
8. B
9. E
10. C

Fill in the blank.

1. trust
2. quasi-contract
3. disclosure
4. unconscionable
5. marriage
6. partnership
7. joint venture
8. putative spouse
9. meretricious
10. welfare
11. willfully
12. public policy
13. cohabit
14. severable
15. palimony

Short answer.

1. household responsibilities during marriage; property ownership during marriage; and support, property division, and related matters in the event of death or divorce

2. the agreement was not signed voluntarily, the agreement is unconscionable, there was not adequate disclosure of assets, the agreement will require one party to depend on welfare benefits for support

3. Such relationships violate the public policy which favors marriage as the primary family relationship. To provide legal remedies to the paries when such a relationship ends encourages people to avoid marriage.

4. If no legal remedy is provided for a party who has contributed to the growth of assets during a nonmarital relationship, the party with the greater assets and income benefits. Our society recognizes the freedom of individuals to make contracts. All citizens should have the opportunity to seek judicial enforcement of their lawful agreements.

5. "Palimony" is a derivative of the word alimony. Alimony is support which may be awarded to a spouse as part of a divorce proceeding. "Palimony" implies that there was a marriage. It is a misnomer to apply this term in cases where no marriage relationship existed.

6. The terms of an express contract may be written or clearly discussed between the parties. An implied contract is one which was not written or openly discussed, but which arises from the situation in which the parties find themselves.

7. They are older, may have families by a previous marriage, have accumulated assets prior to marriage, or have an interest in a family-owned business.

8. In order to willfully waive rights to another's assets, there must be substantial knowledge of the character and value of the assets.

9. an unlawful or immoral sexual relationship

10. Divorce is no longer difficult to obtain. Society recognizes that marriages fail and no one should be required to stay in an unhappy marriage. It is unlikely that a person would want to end a successful marriage merely because a contract expresses the terms of a favorable property settlement or support payment.

Chapter 4

THE FORMATION OF CEREMONIAL MARRIAGES AND COMMON-LAW MARRIAGES

REVIEW OF CHAPTER:

Laws regulating marriage vary from state to state. In order to enter into a valid ceremonial marriage in many states, couples must obtain a marriage license, wait a designated period of time, participate in a ceremony conducted by an authorized official or clergy member witnessed by one or two individuals, and record the license. Additionally state statutes will impose requirements concerning age, degree of kinship, and legal capacity to marry.

Thirteen states and the District of Columbia allow couples to enter into common law marriage. This requires couples to have legal capacity, to make a present agreement to be married, to cohabit, and to openly present themselves to others as married. Validity of marriage is governed by the laws of the state in which the marriage was entered. Full faith and credit provisions of the U.S. Constitution allow states to recognize a marriage as valid as long as it was valid in the state where the marriage was entered.

Although no state presently recognizes marriages between two members of the same sex, some cities have extended domestic partnership status to unmarried cohabiting individuals who chose to register.

REVIEW QUESTIONS:

Multiple choice.
Select the correct answer from the choices provided.

1. Requirements for a valid ceremonial marriage usually include all of the following except:

    a. marriage license
    b. ceremony performed by authorized person
    c. parental consent
    d. witnesses to the ceremony
    e. no exceptions, all of the above are required

Chapter 4 STUDY GUIDE 23

2. The basic difference between ceremonial marriage and common law marriage is:

   a. common law marriage is not valid; ceremonial marriage is valid
   b. except in cases of death, divorce is required to end a ceremonial marriage; no divorce proceeding is required to end a common law marriage
   c. parties must have legal capacity to enter a ceremonial marriage; capacity is not required for common law marriage
   d. ceremonial marriage requires a ceremony performed by an authorized person; no ceremony is required for common law marriage
   e. children of common law marriage are illegitimate; children of ceremonial marriage are legitimate

3. In most states, if parties to a ceremonial marriage fail to comply with a statutory requirement such as a waiting period or recording the license,

   a. the marriage is still valid
   b. the marriage is invalid
   c. they may have created a common law marriage rather than a ceremonial marriage
   d. they will be subject to criminal penalties
   e. they must have another ceremony

4. Legal capacity to marry refers to:

   a. the parties' age
   b. the parties' mental abilities to understand their actions
   c. whether the parties obtained a marriage license
   d. all of the above
   e. a and b

5. In order to enter a common law marriage, the parties must do all of the following except:

   a. have legal capacity to marry
   b. cohabit for seven years
   c. live together
   d. represent themselves to others as husband and wife
   e. agree to be presently married

6. The portion of the United States Constitution which requires states to recognize the validity of another state's judicial proceedings is the:

   a. Due Process Clause

b. Equal Protection Clause
　　　c. Full Faith and Credit Clause
　　　d. Commerce Clause
　　　e. Conflict of Laws Clause

7. In <u>Baehr v. Lewin</u>, the Supreme Court of Hawaii held that the proper test to be applied in cases which allege a denial of equal protection based on classification by sex is the:

　　　a. strict scrutiny test
　　　b. rational basis test
　　　c. compelling state interest test
　　　d. fundamental right test
　　　e. right to privacy test

8. Determining whether a couple's marriage is valid can be significant in situations involving:

　　　a. pension benefits of the surviving spouse
　　　b. whether the survivor is entitled to inherit under intestate succession
　　　c. citizenship
　　　d. social security benefits
　　　e. all of the above

9. The right of a widow to the lifetime use of land her deceased husband owned during their marriage is:

　　　a. forced share
　　　b. intestate succession
　　　c. unconstitutional
　　　d. dower
　　　e. curtesy

Fill in the blank.
Fill in the blank with a term from Chapter 4.

1. The right of a husband to lifetime use of land his deceased wife owned during the marriage is _____.

2. A marriage that is entered in compliance with formal statutory requirements is a

_____ marriage.

3. The document which couples must acquire prior to being married in a formal ceremony is a _____.

4. A marriage in which the ceremony takes place with one absent party represented by an agent is a _____ marriage.

5. The marriage of two people who agree to be married, cohabit, and hold themselves out as husband and wife even though they did not go through a ceremonial marriage is a _____ marriage.

6. Whether the couple enter into a common law or ceremonial marriage, in order for the marriage to be valid, they must have _____ to marry.

7. An _____ is a legal obstacle that prevents the formation of a valid marriage.

8. Some courts would recognize a marriage as a _____ marriage if it was contracted in good faith without knowledge of an existing impediment.

9. In some cities a document which may be filed by unmarried couples who cohabit, to record their intimate relationship is referred to as a declaration of _____.

10. The clause in the U.S. Constitution which requires states to recognize the validity of other states' judicial actions is the _____ Clause.

11. When someone dies without leaving a valid will, the deceased died _____.

12. A requirement of common law marriage is that the couple live together. When couples live together, they _____.

13. The right of a widow to use one-third of the land her deceased husband owned during the marriage is _____.

14. A designated share of a deceased spouse's estate that goes to the surviving spouse in spite of what was left to the surviving spouse in the will is a _____.

15. Marriage or cohabitation by persons of different races is referred to as

Short answer.
Answer each of the following questions in one or two sentences.

1. List three benefits available to married couples, which are not generally available to unmarried cohabiting couples.

2. Identify three legal issues which might make it necessary to determine the marital statute of a client.

3. List four typical requirements for a ceremonial marriage.

4. What are the four requirements for a common law marriage?

5. What is the impact of the Full Faith and Credit Clause in determining the validity of a marriage?

6. What is the difference between the "strict scrutiny test" and the "rational basis test" in equal protection cases?

7. What is the meant by "conflict of law"?

8. Under what circumstances might a court recognize a putative marriage?

9. What constitutional theories were argued by the plaintiffs in Baehr v. Lewin?

10. What is the privilege for marital communications?

PRACTICE EXERCISES:

1. Assume that you are in a state that recognizes common law marriage. Make a list of the type of evidence (documents, statements, behavior, etc.) that would be relevant to prove the existence of a common law marriage.

2. Locate the statutes in your state which contain requirements for a valid ceremonial marriage. Make a checklist of these requirements. Be sure to include requirements of age and legal capacity as well as the technical requirements such as licenses and witnesses.

3. Locate the statutes in your state regarding bigamy. What is the status of an individual who marries without knowledge that the "spouse" was already married? What is the punishment for bigamy (civil/criminal)? Will both spouses be punished?

4. Research your state's case law and statutory law to answer the following questions:

Has the state in which you live ever officially denied individuals the right to marry?

If so, what categories or groups of people have been affected? (ex. homosexuals, prison inmates, individuals of different races) Are these people presently prohibited from marrying under the laws of your state? If not, when and how did the change occur? (ex. court decision, legislative enactment)

ANSWERS TO REVIEW QUESTIONS:

Multiple choice.

1. C
2. D
3. A
4. E
5. B
6. C
7. A
8. E
9. D

Fill in the blank.

1. curtesy
2. ceremonial
3. marriage license
4. proxy
5. common law
6. legal capacity
7. impediment
8. putative
9. domestic partnership
10. Full Faith and Credit
11. intestate
12. cohabit
13. dower
14. forced share
15. miscegenation

Short answer.

1. family health insurance, filing joint income tax returns, inheritance, pension benefits

2. to determine eligibility for social security survivor benefits, to determine eligibility for intestate

inheritance, to establish citizenship

3.	marriage license, waiting period, ceremony performed by authorized person, witnesses

4.	legal capacity, present intent to be married, cohabiting, holding relationship out to public as husband and wife

5.	The Full Faith and Credit Clause requires states to recognize the validity of the judicial acts of other states. If a marriage is valid under the laws of the state in which it was entered, other states will be required to recognize that marriage as valid.

6.	The strict scrutiny test is applied in equal protection cases in which the class of people treated differently is categorized as a "suspect class", such as race. This test requires the state to show a compelling reason for the different treatment. The rational basis test is applied in equal protection cases in which the class of people treated differently is not a "suspect class." Under this test the state must only show a rational basis or some reasonable policy for the different in treatment.

7.	Many laws vary from state to state. When cases arise which involve laws from two jurisdictions, the inconsistency is considered to be a conflict of law.

8.	Some courts might recognize a putative marriage in a situation where a couple attempted to marry, met the technical requirements for marriage, but an impediment existed which prevented the validity of the marriage, and at least one of the parties was innocent and unaware of the impediment. The innocent party would be considered the putative spouse, entitled to rights of a lawful spouse.

9.	right to privacy, equal protection

10.	Spouses cannot disclose in court any confidential communications that occurred between them during the marriage except in cases where they are suing each other.

Chapter 5

ANNULMENT

REVIEW OF CHAPTER:

Annulment is a court proceeding in which the court declares that a valid marriage never existed. In order to obtain an annulment, a party with standing to bring the action must prove that a situation which existed at the time the "marriage" began caused the "marriage" to be either void or voidable. If the annulment is granted, it is as if the marriage never occurred. However, in most states issues of child support and legitimacy will be decided just as though the parents were married.

Grounds for annulment relate to the parties' intent to marry or capacity to marry. Grounds relating to intent include sham marriage, mental disability, duress, and fraud. Grounds relating to capacity include prior existing marriage, consanguinity and affinity, nonage, and physical disabilities.

REVIEW QUESTIONS:

Multiple choice.
Select the correct answer from the choices provided.

1. Which of the following accurately states a difference between annulment and divorce?

    a. in annulment, the court does not address the issue of child support
    b. in divorce, the court terminates a valid marriage
    c. in annulment, the court terminates a void marriage
    d. in annulment, the court declares that a valid marriage never existed
    e. both b and d

2. Which of the following accurately states a difference between annulment and legal separation?

    a. in annulment, the parties are not free to remarry
    b. in legal separation, the parties are not free to remarry
    c. in legal separation, a valid marriage never existed
    d. in legal separation, the court does not address the issue of child support
    e. both b and c

3. Which of the following have standing to seek annulment of a voidable marriage which resulted from fraud?

   a. the parents of the innocent "spouse"
   b. the innocent "spouse"
   c. either "spouse"
   d. the parents of either "spouse"
   e. none of the above, fraud is not a ground for annulment

4. Even if a marriage is valid in the state in which it was contracted, the couple's domiciliary state may consider the marriage to be void if:

   a. the marriage would have been void if it had been contracted in the domiciliary state
   b. the marriage would have been voidable if it had been contracted in the domiciliary state
   c. the marriage violates a strong public policy of the domiciliary state
   d. all of the above
   e. a and c

5. In order for a marriage to be annulled:

   a. the action must be filed before the marriage is consummated
   b. the action must be filed before the parties cohabit
   c. the action must be based on appropriate grounds
   d. the action must be filed before any children are born
   e. the action must be filed before either spouse dies

6. In most states, if a marriage takes place between persons who lack legal capacity because they are related by consanguinity, the marriage will be:

   a. void
   b. voidable
   c. punished by criminal action
   d. terminated
   e. valid

7. If the parties to a voidable marriage do not seek an annulment, the marriage will be considered:

   a. void
   b. illegal
   c. bigamy

d. valid
e. terminated

8. If a voidable marriage is ratified by the parties, the marriage will be considered:

   a. void
   b. illegal
   c. valid
   d. terminated
   e. none of the above

9. In order for fraud to constitute a ground for annulment, many states require that the fraud relate to:

   a. the party's intent to marry
   b. the essentials of the marriage
   c. the party's capacity to marry
   d. the children of the marriage
   e. the health of the parties

10. Which of the following is a ground for annulment related to the capacity to marry?

    a. age of the parties
    b. fraud
    c. duress
    d. mental disability
    e. all of the above

Fill in the blank.
Fill in the blank with a term from Chapter 5.

1. In order to receive an annulment, the party seeking the annulment must show the court that he or she has the necessary _____, which are acceptable reasons for annulment.

2. The term which refers to relationship by blood between two individuals is _____.

3. The term which refers to relationship by marriage is _____.

Chapter 5 — STUDY GUIDE — 33

4. A marriage that is invalid only if someone challenges it and a court declares it invalid is a _____ marriage.

5. A declaration by a court that parties can live apart even though they are still married to each other is a _____.

6. A marriage that is invalid whether or not a court declares it to be so is a _____ marriage.

7. A party must have _____ in order to be eligible to bring a case seeking relief from a court.

8. _____ is the act of entering a second marriage when a prior marriage is still valid.

9. If a spouse who was induced to marry by fraud learns the truth of the fact and decides to remain in the marriage willingly, the spouse has _____ the marriage.

10. The inability to have sexual intercourse due to an inability to achieve an erection is _____.

11. If someone has been forced or coerced into marrying, that person lacks the required _____ to create a valid marriage.

12. Fraud which concerns aspects of the marriage related to sex and children may meet the _____ test applied by some courts in determining whether a marriage is valid or not.

13. Statutes which address the choice of law applied to determine the validity of a marriage in which the couple travelled to a state other than their home state in order to take advantage of the law of the other state are referred to as _____ statutes.

14. A void marriage which the couple entered into as a joke or without the intent to truly become married is a _____ marriage.

15. A party who is prevented from bringing a legal action because allowing the action would be unfair is _____ from filing suit.

Short answer.
Answer each of the following questions in one or two sentences.

1. What are the differences between a legal annulment and a religious annulment?

2. Explain the potential consequences of applying the "relation back" doctrine to annulment.

3. Under present law what is the status of children born to a couple whose marriage has been annulled?

4. What is the IRS rule concerning previously filed joint income tax returns and annulment?

5. What impact did AIDS testing have on marriage license applicants in Illinois during the first six months of this requirement?

6. Explain two reasons for the existence of mental disability as a ground for annulment?

7. What is the distinction between a void marriage and a voidable marriage?

8. What are the two categories of grounds for annulment?

9. What is the significance of "conflict of law" in an annulment proceeding?

10. What is the significance of "dirty hands" to a party seeking an annulment?

Chapter 5 STUDY GUIDE

PRACTICE EXERCISES:

1. Mark McGee and Carol Armstrong married three years ago. Prior to the marriage Mark assured Carol that he wanted a large family. Six months after they married, Carol learned that Mark was sterile. Mark had known this fact for approximately a year before he met Carol. Carol has finally decided that she no longer wants to be married to Mark and would like to have the marriage annulled.

    You attorney has asked you to research the laws of your state to help determine: a) what grounds are required in order to obtain an annulment, and b) whether Carol will be eligible for annulment. Prepare an interoffice memo in which you respond to this request.

2. In today's society when divorce is easily obtained, some couples seek to have their marriage annulled. Make a list of reasons why a couple would prefer annulment over divorce.

3. Identify two states which border the state in which you live. Locate statutes related to capacity to marry for each of these states. Make a list of the degrees of consanguinity each state prohibits from marrying. Compare these lists with the statute of your state. Are any marriages allowed in either of the bordering states but prohibited in your state? Or vice-versa? What are they?

ANSWERS TO REVIEW QUESTIONS:

Multiple choice.

1. E
2. B
3. B
4. E
5. C
6. A
7. D
8. C
9. B
10. A

Fill in the blank.

1. grounds
2. consanguinity
3. affinity
4. voidable
5. legal separation
6. void
7. standing
8. bigamy
9. ratified
10. impotence
11. intent
12. essentials
13. marriage-evasion
14. sham
15. estopped

Short answer.

1.   A legal annulment is a determination by a court that a marriage is invalid. In order to receive a legal annulment, the party seeking the order must be able to show grounds existed which made the marriage either void or voidable. A legal annulment is not recognized by the church as the equivalent

of a religious annulment. The Catholic church maintains its own system to grant annulments based on canon law.

2. Under the old interpretation of the relation back doctrine, some states treated children as illegitimate and refused to allow for spousal support. This was because no marriage had ever taken place under the retroactive policy.

3. Presently most states consider children to be legitimate regardless of the marriage status of their parents.

4. Taxpayers must refile as single taxpayers if the marriage on which they based their joint return is determined to be void.

5. Illinois applications decreased by 22.5% while applications in neighboring states increased. Only 8 of 70,000 applicants tested positive, resulting in a cost of $312,000. for each positive result.

6. To prevent individuals from marrying who cannot understand the nature of the marriage relationship. To discourage mentally ill individuals from becoming parents.

7. A void marriage is invalid from the start due to a serious defect such as the parties lack capacity to marry. A voidable marriage is technically defective, but will not be considered invalid unless one of the parties to the marriage seeks an annulment.

8. Capacity to marry, intent to marry

9. When couples leave their domiciliary state to marry in another state, or marry and then chance their domiciliary state, courts may have to decide which states' law to apply in an annulment proceeding. State laws differ particularly on questions concerning consanguinity. The result of an annulment proceeding may differ depending on which states' law is applied.

10. A party who has "dirty hands" has done something inappropriate to create the situation which may give rise to grounds for annulment. For example, a party who committed fraud in inducing someone to marry has "dirty hands". The court will prevent this person from seeking an annulment.

Chapter 6

SEPARATION AGREEMENTS: LEGAL ISSUES AND DRAFTING OPTIONS

REVIEW OF CHAPTER:

A separation agreement is a contract between a husband and wife who anticipate divorce. The contract contains terms that cover child custody, child support, property division, maintenance (alimony), and any other terms necessary to complete the separation. Valid separation agreements must comply with the principles of contract law which require the contracting parties to have capacity and to act without fraud, collusion, or duress. The agreement must not violate public policy and must be supported by adequate consideration.

Separation agreements are subject to approval by the court and may be incorporated into the court's divorce decree. Drafting a separation agreement requires complete detailed information concerning the couple's real and personal property. This includes all tangible and intangible assets and debts.

REVIEW QUESTIONS:

Multiple choice.
Select the correct answer from the choices provided.

1. Which of the following are appropriate characteristics of an effective separation agreement?

    a. readable
    b. fair
    c. comprehensive
    d. all of the above
    e. b and c.

2. Terms which are included in separation agreements include all of the following except:

    a. alimony
    b. conduct of the parties during marriage

c. child custody
d. health and life insurance
e. real and personal property division

3. Terms concerning children which might be included in a separation agreement include all of the following except:

   a. who obtains custody
   b. visitation with noncustodial parent
   c. changing child's date of birth
   d. payment of child support
   e. changing child's last name

4. A method of discovery requiring written responses to written questions which is often used to uncover information about financial assets of a party is:

   a. interrogatories
   b. deposition
   c. request for production of documents
   d. informal investigation
   e. a, b, and c

5. A valid separation agreement may not violate public policy by:

   a. containing terms of child custody
   b. containing terms concerning a child's religious training
   c. encouraging a collusive divorce
   d. ending a common law marriage
   e. affecting alimony

6. Consideration for the separation agreement may include all of the following except:

   a. promise to file for divorce
   b. wife's promise to relinquish claims against her husband's state
   c. husband's promise to transfer title to land held in his name alone
   d. wife's promise to transfer joint car title to husband
   e. husband's promise to pay all marital debts

7. If a party who is obligated to pay alimony remarries,

   a. the alimony obligation terminates

b. remaining property division obligations terminate
   c. child support obligations terminate
   d. a and b only
   e. none of the above

8. Alimony payments are:

   a. taxable income to the recipient (payee)
   b. deductible from income of the payor
   c. dischargeable debts in bankruptcy
   d. nondischargeable debts in bankruptcy
   e. a, b, and d

9. Payments to a spouse which are pursuant to a property division are:

   a. taxable income to the recipient (payee)
   b. deductible from income of the payor
   c. generally nondischargeable debts in bankruptcy
   d. generally dischargeable debts in bankruptcy
   e. b and c

Fill in the blank.
Fill in the blank with a term from Chapter 6.

1. When one or both parties travel to another state to obtain a divorce and then return to their original home state, the divorce is called a _____ divorce.

2. A separation agreement which was not entered voluntarily may be declared invalid by a court because the party was _____ into signing the agreement.

3. An exchange of promises or transfer of property is adequate _____ to allow the court to find the agreement to be a valid contract.

4. If a party to divorce anticipates that his or her spouse will file for bankruptcy after the divorce, as a recipient of alimony and property division payments, it is better to classify most of the obligated payments as _____.

5. After a divorce is granted, a court generally does not have power to modify terms of (property

Chapter 6 STUDY GUIDE 41

division/alimony).

6. Payments of alimony, child support, or property division which are due but have not been made are called _____.

7. When a debt is released by a bankruptcy court so that the debt is no longer owed, the debt has been _____.

8. One method of enforcing the terms of a property settlement agreement which has been incorporated into the court's divorce decree is through the court's powers of _____.

9. Another term for alimony which is sometimes used to describe payments made while the parties are still married is _____.

10. A category of personal property that is divisible by the court and has generated considerable controversy is a future _____.

11. Property in which each spouse has a one-half interest because it was acquired during the marriage, regardless of who earned it or who has title to it is _____ property.

12. Property totally owned by one spouse is _____ property.

13. The goal of a court in a common law property state is to achieve _____ of property.

14. In community property states, property acquired during marriage other than by gift or inheritance will be divided so that each spouse receives a _____ share.

15. In common law property states, property acquired during marriage other than by gift or inheritance will be divided so that each spouse receives a _____ share.

Short answer.
Answer each of the following questions in one or two sentences.

1. Explain the difference in property divisions between community property states and common law property states.

2. Identify five major subjects which are addressed in separation agreements.

3. Explain how property items such as houses or automobiles may be divided by a court.

4. What is a Qualified Domestic Relations Order?

5. What is meant by the value of "goodwill" of a business?

6. What is the significance of an indemnification clause in a separation agreement?

7. What is the significance of having a separation agreement incorporated and merged into the court's divorce decree?

8. What is meant by the power of a court to "modify" terms of an agreement?

9. Under what circumstances will alimony payments terminate?

10. Identify four factors a court will consider in awarding alimony.

PRACTICE EXERCISES:

Chapter 6　　　　　　　　　　　　　　STUDY GUIDE　　　　　　　　　　　　　　43

1. Assume that Bill and Becky live in a community property state and are in the process of divorcing. Using the following items and values of property, make two lists (one for Bill and one for Becky) which reflect a 50/50 split between the parties. Determine the total value of property to be awarded to each party. Each list should also include the outstanding debts which each party will be obligated to pay.

    a. the family home; present market value = $150,000, outstanding debt = $90,000.
    b. 1994 GMC truck; present market value = $20,000, outstanding debt = $15,000.
    c. 1992 Honda Accord; present market value = $9,500, outstanding debt = $5,500.
    d. household furniture; present value = $3,000, no debt.
    e. big screen TV and entertainment center; present value = $2,000, no debt.
    f. Certificates of Deposit; present value = $2,500.
    g. cash in checking and savings accts. = $9,500.

2. Assume that Bill and Becky live in a common law property state and are in the process of divorcing. Use the same list of property values and debts in Exercise #1, above to make two lists which reflect a "fair and equitable" distribution of assets and debts.

3. Assume that Bill and Becky own real property (the family home and a lake house). They are unable to agree on the value of these assets and it is necessary to have the property appraised. Use any available resources such as library materials, on line services, telephone directories, etc. to make a list of possible experts who could assist in the appraisal process. Identify each potential expert by the type of business or service category provided, individual or business name, address and telephone number (if available).

4. Contact two experts you identified in Exercise #3, above. Determine what each expert would charge to conduct a real estate appraisal and to testify in court concerning his or her opinion of property valuation.

ANSWERS TO REVIEW QUESTIONS:

Multiple choice.

1. D
2. B
3. C
4. A
5. C
6. A
7. E
8. E
9. C

Fill in the blank.

1. migratory
2. coerced
3. consideration
4. alimony
5. property division
6. arrears
7. discharged
8. contempt
9. spousal support or separate maintenance
10. pension
11. community
12. separate
13. equitable distribution
14. 50/50 or equal
15. fair or equitable

Short answer.

1. In community property states, property acquired during marriage other than by gift or inheritance and appreciation of property acquired during marriage is split 50/50 between the spouses unless they agree otherwise. In common law states, the same property would be divided so that each spouse gets a fair (equitable) share, which may or may not be equal.

2. child custody, child support, property division, alimony, debts

3. A single item such as a house or car cannot be divided "in kind", that is the house cannot be split down the middle. These items may be distributed to one party and an item or combination of items and cash of offsetting value distributed to the other party.

4. a court order that allows a nonemployee (former spouse) to receive a portion of an employee's pension benefits directly from the pension plan administrator in order to satisfy a marital obligation

5. the intangible assets of a business such as reputation and customer following

6. When a court orders one party to be responsible for payment of debts which were incurred by the couple during marriage, the creditor is not barred from seeking payment from the other party. An indemnification clause will allow the second party to seek reimbursement from the first party in the event the second party pays the creditor.

7. The decree can be enforced by the court's powers of contempt and some terms of the decree may be modifiable by the court.

8. power to change the terms of the original agreement in the event that a change in circumstances merits the modification

9. death of either spouse, remarriage of payee, other conditions which may be contained in the agreement

10. length of marriage, age of the payee, need of the payee, property division, income of the parties

Chapter 7

CHILD CUSTODY

REVIEW OF CHAPTER:

Child custody includes legal custody and physical custody. A court may award sole custody or joint custody to the parents of the child or to a non-parent. In resolving custody disputes, courts apply the standard of the best interest of the child. Relevant factors the courts consider include stability, the child's needs, and existing emotional ties. Presumptions concerning child custody such as the tender years doctrine have been generally rejected.

Unless a reason exits to limit parental contact, courts usually grant liberal visitation rights to the noncustodial parent. Occasionally visitation is granted to other individuals such as grandparents. The state Uniform Child Custody Jurisdiction Act and the federal Parental Kidnapping Prevention Act were enacted to reduce forum shopping and child snatching by parents who are dissatisfied with an existing custody order. Child custody orders may be modified by the court when changed circumstances make it necessary.

REVIEW QUESTIONS:

Multiple choice.
Select the correct answer from the choices provided.

1. In custody disputes, to determine where a child will reside as well as who will make decisions about the child's upbringing, a court will make an award of:

    a. sole custody and joint custody
    b. parental custody and third-party custody
    c. legal custody and physical custody
    d. split custody and shared custody
    e. physical custody and psychological custody

2. The right of a custodial parent to make decisions concerning a child's health, education, religion, and discipline is:

a. legal custody
b. physical custody
c. the tender years doctrine
d. the primary caregiver presumption
e. visitation

3. Circumstances that should be considered by the parties in negotiating a custody agreement include all of the following except:

a. the age and health of the child
b. the age and health of the parents
c. the parent with whom the child has the strongest emotional attachment
d. the parent who earns the highest income
e. the method of resolving future disputes concerning custody

4. If divorcing parents have been involved in an extensive dispute concerning custody of the children, and the judge finds that parent "A" is likely to attempt to alienate the children from parent "B," but that parent "A" earns a substantially higher income than parent "B", which of the following custody awards would you expect the court to make?

a. third-party custody
b. sole legal and physical custody to parent "A" with no visitation for parent "B"
c. sole legal and physical custody to parent "A" with reasonable visitation to parent "B"
d. sole legal and physical custody to parent "B" and no visitation for parent "A"
e. sole legal custody and physical custody to parent "B," with specific visitation terms for parent "A"

5. If divorcing parents have different religious practices, a judge, who is making a custody decision, is lawfully permitted to consider the parents' religious beliefs to the extent that:

a. one parent's religious beliefs are more "conventional" than the other
b. one parent's religious beliefs may be dangerous or detrimental to the child's health
c. one parent's religious beliefs are the same as those of the judge
d. the child, age 3, expresses an interest in one religion over the other
e. none of the above, a judge may not consider religion in deciding custody

6. If divorcing parents are involved in a contested custody dispute, and it is proven that one parent physically or sexually abused the children before the divorce, the court will most likely:

a. limit the abusive parent to supervised visitation with the children
b. deny custody to the non-abusive parent
c. deny visitation to the parent who accused the other parent of abuse
d. disregard the abuse as a factor in determining custody
e. award custody to the abusive parent

7. If parents have shown a serious inability to agree on custody and visitation, it would be a good idea for the final custody terms to include:

a. reasonable visitation terms for the non-custodial parent
b. specific visitation terms for the non-custodial parent
c. joint legal and physical custody
d. third party custody
e. a tender years presumption

8. Of the several factors that the court considers in making a custody decision, the most significant is generally:

a. the parents' religion
b. the child's age
c. the child's wishes
d. the recommendations of expert witnesses
e. stability

9. A non-custodial parent asks the court to consider a request for modification of custody (to change custody from the present custodial parent to the present non-custodial parent) based on a significant change in circumstances. In which of the following situations is it most likely that the request will be granted?

a. the non-custodial parent is promoted to a higher paying job
b. the custodial parent plans to take the children on an eight-week vacation to England next summer
c. the custodial parent is permanently relocating to a remote Pacific island
d. the custodial parent is permanently relocating to a town that is 35 miles from his/her present home
e. the non-custodial parent takes a new job that will require frequent overnight travel

10. Under the Uniform Child Custody Jurisdiction Act, in which of the following situations is a court most likely to decline to accept jurisdiction of a custody matter?

a. the state is the "home state" of the child
b. the parent who makes the request for hearing has secretly brought the child to this state in violation of the original custody order

c. the parent who makes the request for hearing has "clean hands" and no other state has jurisdiction
d. the child has been physically abandoned in the state
e. the state is not the home state of the child, but the child and parents have a significant connection to this state and substantial evidence about the child exists in this state

Fill in the blank.
Fill in the blank with a term from Chapter 7.

1. The right and duty to make decisions concerning a child's health, education, religion, and discipline is _____ custody.

2. The parent with whom the child resides is the parent who has _____ custody.

3. When only one parent has both legal custody and physical custody of a child, this parent has been awarded _____ custody.

4. An individual who is appointed by the court to represent the child's interests during litigation is known as a _____.

5. In the years following the mid-1800's, courts routinely awarded very young children to their mothers. This judicial preference is called the _____ doctrine.

6. Many modern courts have begun to follow a presumption that custody should go to the parent who has been most responsible for taking care of the child's needs. This judicial preference is known as the _____ presumption.

7. The parent who does not have legal custody of the child is the _____ parent.

8. When parents share legal custody of a child, they have _____ custody.

9. The overriding standard that courts must follow when deciding child custody cases is _____.

10. The process of meeting with a third party (other than a judge) who will help the parties reach an acceptable resolution of a dispute is _____.

11. If the parties cannot agree on a custody matter, and the issue is disputed or challenged in court, the case is said to be a _____ matter.

12. When a court grants a request for a change in custody after an initial custody order has been made, the court issues a _____ of the earlier order.

13. A "nonparent" who has formed a close relationship with a child may be involved in a custody dispute with a child's biological parent. This "nonparent" is often called a _____ parent.

14. The practice of going from one state court to another in an attempt to seek a favorable court ruling on custody is known as _____.

15. The Uniform Child Custody Jurisdiction Act refers to the state where a child has lived for at least six consecutive months as the _____ state of the child.

Short answer.
Answer each of the following questions in one or two sentences.

1. What is the significance of "the best interests of the child" in custody disputes?

2. What particular custody problems did the states attempt to address by enacting the Uniform Child Custody Jurisdiction Act?

3. In considering custody and visitation matters, what significance might a judge place on a parent's pre-divorce extramarital affair?

4. Why is an allegation of child abuse in a custody case sometimes called a "terror weapon?"

5. How has the primary caregiver presumption affected custody decisions?

Chapter 7   STUDY GUIDE   51

6. How does mediation differ from litigation in custody disputes?

7. What factors concerning a child's family relationships and home environment do courts consider when deciding custody cases?

8. Under what general circumstances will a court consider a motion to modify a custody order?

9. Explain the difference between "reasonable visitation" and "specific visitation."

10. Under what circumstances might a court order supervised visitation?

PRACTICE EXERCISES:

1. Bill and Becky have been divorced for four years. When the divorce was granted, the judge approved a separation agreement in which Bill and Becky outlined a plan for joint legal custody of the two children, Michael and Taylor. At the time Michael was 3 and Taylor was 5 years old. Until three months ago Bill and Becky lived only 12 miles from each other. The children spent school nights with Becky and every other Friday and Saturday nights with Bill. Six months ago Becky's employer transferred her to a city 350 miles away, and Bill has only seen the children three times since she moved.

   Draft a Motion to Modify Custody of the children to be filed on Bill's behalf. Assume that Bill seeks sole legal custody of both children.

2. Assume that your attorney will represent Becky in the modification proceeding (review the scenario in Practice Exercise #1, above). You have been asked to conduct the client intake interview. Becky would like to continue the joint custody arrangement, but understands the difficulty involved in making decisions with the children's father who is 350 miles away. She

does not want the court to grant sole custody to Bill under any circumstances.

You may assume that your attorney represented Becky in the original divorce proceeding, and you have already verified at the start of this interview that the vital statistic and background information in your file is still correct. Prepare a checklist of the questions you would ask Becky concerning the modification.

3. Locate the statute in your state that identifies the available forms of child custody, (joint custody, sole custody, etc.). Does the statute establish a preferred form of custody?

    a. If so, what is it? Locate at least three court decisions from your state in which the judge decided a custody dispute. How many of them followed the preferred form of custody expressed in the statute? What reasons do you find in each opinion to explain why the court awarded custody as it did?

    b. If your state's statute does not express a preferred form of custody, locate at least three court decisions and determine what form of custody was awarded by the court in each. What reasons do you find in the opinions to explain why the court made each of those decisions?

4. Assume that your attorney has agreed to represent a homosexual parent who seeks custody of a child. Draft a checklist of the questions you would ask this client in an initial interview.

5. Research your state's criminal statutes concerning parental kidnapping or interference with child custody. What particular acts of this nature carry criminal penalties? How are these acts classified (as felonies, misdemeanors, etc.)? What type of punishment is provided for conviction?

Chapter 7 — STUDY GUIDE — 53

ANSWERS TO REVIEW QUESTIONS:

Multiple choice.

1. C
2. A
3. D
4. E
5. B
6. A
7. B
8. E
9. C
10. B

Fill in the blank.

1. legal
2. physical
3. sole
4. guardian ad litem
5. tender years
6. primary caregiver
7. non-custodial
8. joint
9. the best interests of the child
10. mediation
11. contested
12. modification
13. psychological
14. forum shopping
15. home

Short answer.

1. This is the standard used by the court in deciding custody matters. It requires the court to

consider the impact a custody arrangement will have on the child.

2.   The UCCJA was enacted to address questions of a court's original jurisdiction and jurisdiction to modify custody orders from another state's court. Jurisdictional problems arose in situations in which parents removed children from one state and attempted to have a court in a different state hear questions of child custody.

3.   In considering the morality and lifestyle of a parent, the court can evaluate the impact (if any) an extramarital affair has had on the child.

4.   A parent who has abused a child is unlikely to receive custody of the child. Therefore, some parents have used an allegation of abuse (which may not always be proven) to defeat the other parent's request for custody or visitation.

5.   Theoretically the primary caregiver presumption gives both parents an equal chance at being awarded custody without regard to gender. In practice, however, mothers still receive custody in approximately 70% of the cases.

6.   A mediator assists the parents in reaching a mutually acceptable decision. The mediator does not make the decision for the parents. In contested litigation the judge makes the decision for the parents.

7.   Factors concerning a child's family and home which the court will consider when deciding custody include: stability and continuity in the child's living arrangement; availability of parents to respond to the child's day-to-day needs; closeness of emotional ties between the parents and the child.

8.   The court will consider a motion to modify a) when there has been a significant change in circumstances since the earlier order was entered, OR b) when there are relevant facts which were not available to the court at the time of the original order.

9.   "Reasonable visitation" usually means that the visiting parent will spend time with the child on an unspecified ("reasonable") schedule. Generally this includes visits on alternate weekends and every other holiday. "Specific visitation" expressly establishes definite dates and times for visitation.

10.   A court might order supervised visitation if it found that a parent was incapable of properly caring for a child or if the child was in danger of being harmed or abducted by the parent during visitation.

Chapter 8

CHILD SUPPORT

REVIEW OF CHAPTER:

Child support is an obligation of both parents, regardless of marital status. Although the parents may negotiate an agreement regarding child support, the court must decide whether the amount is appropriate. In reviewing a negotiated amount or in ordering child support without a recommendation from the parents, courts use federally mandated Child Support Guidelines as a rebuttable presumption of the correct amount. Each state's guidelines present a method of calculation based on both parents' incomes, number or children, and age of children.

Child support payments may be enforced in a variety of ways including civil contempt actions, criminal prosecutions, income withholding, tax refund intercepts, QDROs, QMCSOs, and credit clouding.

REVIEW QUESTIONS:

Multiple choice.
Select the correct answer from the choices provided.

1. Parents may negotiate and agree to an amount of child support payments. This agreement will be:

    a. binding on the court
    b. binding on the children
    c. subject to approval by the court
    d. subject to approval by the children
    e. both c and d

2. In order for a court to issue a child support order which is binding on an individual defendant:

    a. the defendant must appear in court in person
    b. the court must have personal jurisdiction over the defendant
    c. the defendant must be domiciled in the state in which the court is located
    d. the court must apply the "long arm" statute

e. the court must have personal jurisdiction over the child

3. A state statute which enables a court to exercise personal jurisdiction over a nonresident is:

   a. unconstitutional
   b. URESA
   c. QDRO
   d. a long-arm statute
   e. not applicable to child support proceedings

4. Factors which state courts consider in determining the amount of chid support include:

   a. the child's age
   b. state child support guidelines
   c. fault of either parent in causing the divorce
   d. a and b
   e. b and c

5. Existing child support orders may be modified by a court:

   a. when a substantial change of circumstances has occurred since the existing order was entered
   b. if the obligor becomes voluntarily impoverished
   c. when the obligor receives an increase in salary
   d. if the recipient remarries
   e. when the cost of living index increases

6. A modification of an existing child support order is effective to modify:

   a. future payments
   b. arrearage
   c. payments which became due after the date that notice of the petition to modify was given to the obligor
   d. all of the above
   e. a and c only

7. Child support payments are:

   a. taxed as income to the recipient
   b. deductible from income of the obligor
   c. not taxed as income to the recipient

d. taxed as income to the child
e. both a and b

8. State agencies established by Congress as part of the Social Security Act for the purpose of child support collection are known as:

   a. Title IV-D agencies
   b. AFDC agencies
   c. QDRO agencies
   d. QMSRO agencies
   e. none of the above

9. The State Parent Locator Service may be helpful in locating an absent child support obligor through information such as:

   a. the obligor's social security number
   b. the obligor's employer
   c. the number of children the obligor has parented
   d. the name of obligor's current spouse
   e. a, b, and d

10. Statistics show that the most effective means of child support enforcement is through:

    a. tax refund intercept
    b. wage withholding
    c. criminal contempt
    d. assignment of AFDC benefits
    e. a and d

Fill in the blank.
Fill in the blank with a term from Chapter 8.

1. A proceeding in which the marriage is terminated, but the court does not decide other issues such as child support, custody, or property division is known as a _____ _____.

2. A custodial parent who receives AFDC payments will be required to _____ to the state his or her right to receive child support payments from an absent parent.

3. A method of enforcing child support obligations in which the obligor is found to have violated a court order is known as _____.

4. Child support payments which have come due, but have not been paid are _____.

5. A parent who has been threatened with violence by the defendant in a child support enforcement proceeding may choose to seek a _____ from the court.

6. A court order that a group health plan provide insurance benefits for the child of a parent who is covered under the plan is a _____.

7. A method of collecting child support in which the obligor's property under the control of another (ex. bank accounts, income) is taken in order to provide child support payments is known as _____.

8. A method of enforcing child support in which the obligor's nonpayment is reported to a credit bureau is known as _____.

9. The most effective means of enforcing child support orders is through _____.

10. TRIP, a method of collecting child support payments, stands for _____.

11. The duty to support children belongs to _____ parents.

12. Federal law mandated that states enact _____ _____ to be used by the court as a rebuttable presumption in determining the correct amount of child support.

13. The place where a person is physically present with the intent to make a permanent home is his or her _____.

14. A law that gives a state court personal jurisdiction over a nonresident based on purposeful contact with the state is a _____ statute.

Short answer.

Chapter 8 STUDY GUIDE 59

Answer each of the following questions in one or two sentences.

1. Of the 6.2 million parents with child support awards or agreements, approximately what percent receive full or partial payments? What percent receive no payments?

2. What factors do courts consider in determining an appropriate amount of child support?

3. What is the significance of a "long-arm" statute in making a child support order?

4. How do state courts use child support guidelines in determining the amount of a child support award?

5. Name two circumstances under which a party may request a modification of an existing child support order.

6. What is meant by "potential income", and how could it impact a court's child support order?

7. Identify and explain four methods of enforcing child support orders.

8. Name two uniform acts which may be used by a custodial parent in one state to obtain and enforce child support in another state.

9. Explain the process of civil contempt for enforcement of child support.

10. Give three examples of "necessaries."

PRACTICE EXERCISES:

1. Obtain a copy of your state's child support guidelines. Use the figures below to calculate the correct child support obligation for each parent. Although you do not have amounts for all information which may be requested on the guideline form (such as child care costs, medical expenses, etc.), you may either use zeros or make a realistic estimate of these amounts.

   Monthly gross income: father, $1900.
                             mother, $1100.

   Health insurance premiums
   for children: father, $45.
                             mother, 0

   Ages of children: son, age 10
                             daughter, age 7

2. Assume that your firm's client is a self-employed salesperson. In order to calculate an appropriate amount for child support, we must determine the client's gross monthly income amount. Make a checklist of documents, records, receipts, etc. that you would like the client to bring to the office in order to determine the client's income.

3. Assume that your firm's client wants to prevent the court from modifying an initial child support order on behalf of her two minor children. The children's father has been employed as attorney in a medium-size law firm for the past seven years. His gross income last year was $95,000. Earlier this year he decided to become a science fiction novelist and has begun to practice law only part time. He has not completed his first novel, and his current gross income from part-time employment is $25,000. He requests a reduction in child support on the basis of his lower income.

   Your attorney will take the position that: 1) the father's reduction in income is not a substantial change in circumstances to allow the court to entertain a motion to modify; and 2) the father's imputed or potential income (which remains at $95,000) should be used to calculate child support.

Locate caselaw from your state which would be helpful to your attorney in preparing for this case.

ANSWERS TO REVIEW QUESTIONS:

Multiple choice.

1. C
2. B
3. D
4. D
5. A
6. E
7. C
8. A
9. E
10. B

Fill in the blank.

1. divisible divorce
2. assign
3. contempt
4. arrearage
5. protective order
6. Qualified Medical Child Support Order (QMCSO)
7. garnishment
8. credit clouding
9. wage withholding
10. Tax Refund Intercept Program (TRIP)
11. both
12. child support guidelines
13. domicile
14. long-arm statute

Short answer.

1. full payments, 50%; partial payments, 25%; no payments, 25%

2. child support guidelines, financial resources and earning potential of both parents, age of child, child's standard of living before the divorce, child's need and capacity for education, financial needs of

noncustodial parent, noncustodial parent's obligation to support others

3. A court must have personal jurisdiction before it can make a child support order binding an individual defendant. If the defendant no longer lives in the state where the court is located, but has had significant contacts with the state (such as having lived in the state while married), the court may use the long-arm statute to obtain personal jurisdiction over the defendant.

4. Child support guidelines provide a formula for calculating an appropriate amount of child support based on factors such as both parents' income. The guideline amount is a rebuttable presumption of the correct amount of support and will be the amount of the award unless it would result in an inequitable result to the parties or to the child.

5. A modification may be considered when a substantial change in circumstances has occurred since the existing order was made. Under federal law a review may be requested every three years to make sure it complies with child support guidelines.

6. Potential income is an amount that could be earned by an individual who is currently not earning an income in that amount. The potential income is estimated by reviewing employment opportunities for someone with the party's education, training, and experience. The court may use this potential income in determining child support in situations where the party has voluntarily chosen to reduce or eliminate his or her income.

7. contempt, tax refund intercept, wage withholding, credit clouding

8. Uniform Reciprocal Enforcement of Support Act (URESA), Uniform Interstate Family Support Act (UIFSA)

9. The obligor is brought before the court in a civil (not criminal) proceeding. If the court finds that the obligor has the ability to pay, but has chosen not to pay court ordered child support payments, the obligor may be placed in jail until an agreement is reached concerning the payment of child support arrearage and future amounts.

10. food, clothing, housing, medical care, education

Chapter 9

DIVORCE, JUDICIAL SEPARATION, AND SEPARATE MAINTENANCE

REVIEW OF CHAPTER:

Grounds for divorce can be categorized as "fault" or "no-fault" grounds. Fault grounds include desertion, adultery, and cruelty. Statutory "no-fault" grounds vary from state to state, but are frequently expressed in terms such as "incompatibility," "irreconcilable differences," "living apart," and "irretrievable breakdown." A party who chooses not to end the marriage, but who seeks an order from the court allowing him or her to live separately from a spouse may obtain a judicial separation or an order of separate maintenance. In these proceedings the court can award spousal support, custody, and child support.

REVIEW QUESTIONS:

Multiple choice.
Select the correct answer from the choices provided.

1. Common "no-fault" grounds for divorce include all except:

   a. desertion
   b. irreconcilable differences
   c. incompatibility
   d. living apart
   e. irretrievable breakdown

2. Common "fault" grounds for divorce include:

   a. living apart
   b. cruelty
   c. adultery
   d. incompatibility
   e. b and c

Chapter 9 STUDY GUIDE 65

3. In 1969 the first "no-fault" divorce law in the United States was enacted in:

   a. New York
   b. Nevada
   c. California
   d. Colorado
   e. New Mexico

4. In the period of the "fault" system of divorce, reasons given for recognizing the need for reform in divorce laws included:

   a. most divorces were uncontested
   b. collusion between the parties
   c. the system encouraged migratory divorces
   d. all of the above
   e. a and b

5. The "no-fault" ground which requires a particular condition to exist between the parties for a specified time period is:

   a. desertion
   b. living apart
   c. incompatibility
   d. irreconcilable differences
   e. cruelty

6. When a spouse has disappeared for a certain period of time, a presumption that the missing spouse is dead arises under the:

   a. Elizabeth Arden defense
   b. Enoch Light defense
   c. Enoch Arden defense
   d. desertion defense
   e. none of the above

7. Defenses to fault grounds for divorce include:

   a. provocation
   b. collusion
   c. marital discord

d. adultery
e. a and b

8. In some faiths, couples who obtain a legal divorce may also seek a religious divorce in order to be free to remarry within the faith. In the Jewish faith, the wife receives a bill of divorcement from her husband. This document is called a:

   a. get
   b. agunah
   c. talak
   d. beth din
   e. none of the above

9. A judicial separation is also known as a:

   a. legal separation
   b. divorce
   c. dissolution
   d. limited divorce
   e. a and d

10. A characteristic of a judicial separation decree in many states is that:

    a. it can be converted into a separate maintenance decree
    b. it can be converted into a divorce
    c. it can not award alimony
    d. it is granted in a religious ceremony
    e. it does not require the parties to establish grounds

Fill in the blank.
Fill in the blank with a term from Chapter 9.

1. Legally acceptable reasons for seeking a divorce are called _____.

2. Reasons for granting a divorce that do not require proof that either spouse committed marital wrongs are _____.

3. A declaration by a court that parties can live separately even though they are still married to

Chapter 9 STUDY GUIDE 67

each other is a decree of _____.

4. _____ exists when a spouse justifiably leaves the marital home because of unacceptable conduct by the spouse who stayed home.

5. The _____ is the person who allegedly had voluntary sexual intercourse with a spouse charged with adultery.

6. When states enacted divorce reform laws, some adopted the term _____ in place of the term divorce.

7. The breakdown of the marriage to the point where no reasonable hope of reconciliation exists defines the "no-fault" ground known as _____.

8. The no-fault ground of _____ describes the impossibility of the parties living together because of severe conflicts or personality differences.

9. The no-fault ground of _____ exists when spouses voluntarily live separately for a designated period of consecutive time.

10. A divorce request which is not disputed or challenged is _____.

11. A _____ divorce is one which is obtained in a state to which one or both parties traveled before returning to their original state.

12. In some states, a decree of _____ may be converted into a divorce decree.

13. _____ is voluntary sexual intercourse between a married person and someone to whom he or she is not married.

14. _____ is a tort committed by a person who has sexual relations with the plaintiff's spouse.

15. Another word for desertion is _____.

Short answer.
Answer each of the following questions in one or two sentences.

1. What is the major difference between "fault" and "no-fault" grounds for divorce?

2. Why do some couples seek a religious divorce in addition to a legal divorce?

3. What is the major difference between divorce and a judicial separation?

4. What is the difference between a "separation" and a "judicial separation"?

5. What is meant by the "conversion feature" of a decree of separate maintenance?

6. Why is an action for separate maintenance sometimes referred to as an "action for support"?

7. How are separate maintenance decrees enforced?

8. What reasons are given to explain the need for divorce reform?

9. List the three primary fault grounds for divorce.

10. List the three major no-fault grounds for divorce.

PRACTICE EXERCISES:

1. Make a list of the grounds for divorce available in your state. Include fault and no-fault grounds.

2. Identify the statutory language used to allege fault grounds for divorce available in your state. Locate at least three court decisions from your state in which an allegation of fault was used to obtain a divorce. Do the cases reflect the exact language used in the statute? If not, how do the cases explain, broaden or apply the statutory language? If appropriate, add these allegations as examples of fault grounds to the list you created in Practice Exercise #1.

3. Using the "no-fault" ground for divorce available in your state, draft a paragraph which would allege this ground in a petition for divorce to be filed on behalf your law firm's client.

ANSWERS TO REVIEW QUESTIONS:

Multiple choice.

1. A
2. E
3. C
4. D
5. B
6. C
7. E
8. A
9. E
10. B

Fill in the blank.

1. grounds
2. no-fault grounds
3. judicial separation
4. constructive desertion
5. co-respondent
6. dissolution
7. irreconcilable differences
8. incompatibility
9. living apart
10. uncontested
11. migratory
12. separate maintenance (also judicial separation)
13. adultery
14. criminal conversation
15. abandonment

Short answer.

1. Fault grounds require proof that one spouse has committed some misdeed or marital misconduct to cause the divorce. No-fault grounds merely require proof that the marriage is not working.

2. In some faiths, a religious divorce is necessary in order for the parties to be free to remarry. Some faiths do not recognize legal divorce.

3. Divorce terminates the marriage. Judicial separations do not end the marriage relationship.

4. "Separation" is a term commonly used by lay people to describe the situation of physically living apart. "Judicial separation" is an enforceable court decree which permits the parties to live apart and, when appropriate, includes orders regarding child custody and support.

5. In some states, a decree of separate maintenance may be converted by a court into a decree of divorce after some time of separation.

6. An action for separate maintenance is primarily for the purpose of having the court order enforceable support or alimony.

7. Separate maintenance decrees are enforced the same way divorce decrees are: contempt, execution.

8. The system was considered irrelevant and it encouraged fraud. Most divorces were uncontested, and some parties would engage in collusion to obtain divorces on required grounds.

9. adultery, cruelty, desertion

10. living apart, incompatibility, irreconcilable differences/irretrievable breakdown

Chapter 10

DIVORCE PROCEDURE

REVIEW OF CHAPTER:
For a court to have in rem jurisdiction to grant a divorce, one or both parties must be domiciled within the state. In order for a court to order alimony, child support, or property division, the court must also have personal jurisdiction over the defendant. Valid orders from one state court are enforceable in other states under the Full Faith and Credit clause of Article IV of the U.S. Constitution.

Enforcement methods include civil contempt, execution, garnishment, attachment, QDRO, QMCSO, URESA, and UIFSA.

REVIEW QUESTIONS:

Multiple choice.
Select the correct answer from the choices provided.

1. The state where a person is living with the intention to make that state his or her permanent home is the person's:

    a. residence
    b. domicile
    c. place of birth
    d. temporary domicile

2. In order for a court to grant a divorce and issue binding orders concerning maintenance and property division:

    a. the court must have in rem jurisdiction over the marriage
    b. the court must have personal jurisdiction over the defendant
    c. the court must have subject matter jurisdiction over the divorce proceeding
    d. all of the above
    e. a and c only

3. Statutes which allow courts to exercise jurisdiction over a non-resident defendant who previously lived in the state while married to the party who is seeking a divorce, are known as:

   a. long-arm statutes
   b. due process statutes
   c. service of process statutes
   d. in rem statutes
   e. subject matter statutes

4. A divorce in which the defendant does not appear and does not dispute any of the issues raised by the petition may be characterized as a:

   a. default divorce
   b. ex parte divorce
   c. uncontested divorce
   d. bilateral divorce
   e. a, b, and c

5. A court which has subject matter jurisdiction and in rem jurisdiction, but does not have personal jurisdiction over the defendant can:

   a. grant a divorce
   b. not grant a divorce
   c. award maintenance and divide property
   d. award child support
   e. a, c, and d

6. In some states, a procedural difference between divorce cases and other civil cases is that:

   a. no discovery is allowed in divorce cases, but is allowed in most other civil cases
   b. no judge presides over divorce cases, but does preside over most other civil cases
   c. no jury trial is permitted in divorce cases, but is permitted in most other civil cases
   d. no service of process is required in divorce cases, but is required in most other civil cases
   e. both a and c

7. The privilege for marital communications:

   a. prevents a spouse from testifying about confidential communications between the spouses which occurred during the marriage
   b. does not apply in divorce proceedings between the spouses
   c. does not apply in criminal cases

d. both a and b
   e. all of the above

8. A form of alternative dispute resolution that is frequently used in divorce cases to reach a mutual agreement concerning child custody and visitation is:

   a. arbitration
   b. mediation
   c. interlocutory decrees
   d. rent-a-judge
   e. ADR

9. A writ of execution is a method of enforcing a court order through the act of:

   a. garnishing the debtor's wages
   b. placing the debtor in jail
   c. seizing and selling the debtor's property
   d. shooting the debtor
   e. modifying the original court order

10. The type of court order which requires a parent to include the children on a group health plan is known as a:

    a. QMCSO
    b. QDRO
    c. URESA
    d. UIFSA
    e. none of the above

Fill in the blank.
Fill in the blank with a term from Chapter 10.

1. A divorce which is not disputed or challenged by the defendant is _____.

2. In most states, a court does not have in rem jurisdiction to dissolve the marriage unless at least one of the parties has established a _____ in the state.

3. When only one party appears at the divorce hearing, the proceeding is referred to as an

Chapter 10　　　　　　　　　　STUDY GUIDE　　　　　　　　　　75

_____ proceeding.

4. A challenge to a divorce decision which is made in a normal appeal of the trial court's judgment is a _____ attack.

5. A challenge to a divorce decision which is made in a proceeding outside the normal appeal process is a _____ attack.

6. The power of the court to hear cases of a particular type is _____ jurisdiction.

7. The initial pleading which is filed by the party who seeks to obtain a divorce is called a _____.

8. The court's formal notice ordering the defendant to appear in court and respond to the plaintiff's allegations is a _____.

9. A party who represents herself in a divorce action is proceeding _____.

10. Of all the courts in a state which might have jurisdiction over a divorce action, the particular court or county where the action is heard (usually based on the domicile of the plaintiff) is the court with _____.

11. _____ is a method of discovery which consists of written questions sent to one party before the trial.

12. _____ is a method of discovery which allows the requesting party to inspect or copy documents or other tangible things such as tax returns or business records.

13. An action for establishment and enforcement of child support which is initiated in one state, but in which the actual hearing occurs in a different state in which the defendant resides, may be filed under statutes known as _____ or _____.

14. The portion of Article IV of the U.S. Constitution which requires states to recognize judicial proceedings of other states is known as the _____ Clause.

15. A method of enforcing a court order which allows an ex-spouse to receive a portion of an employee's pension benefit is through a _____.

Short answer.
Answer each of the following questions in one or two sentences.

1. What is the primary distinction between personal jurisdiction and in rem jurisdiction?

2. What is the primary distinction between subject matter jurisdiction and venue?

3. What is meant by an order pendent lite?

4. What is the purpose of a "long-arm" statute?

5. What is the role of a guardian ad litem?

6. Identify three methods of enforcing a court's judgment regarding division of property or maintenance.

7. What is the significance of a Qualified Medical Child Support Order?

8. Identify three methods of discovery which would help a party obtain information about marital assets or debts prior to trial.

9. Under what circumstances may URESA or UIFSA be useful to a parent seeking enforcement of child support?

10. What kind of jurisdiction is a court exercising when it makes an order requiring a defendant to pay maintenance or child support?

PRACTICE EXERCISES:

1. Locate a case in your state in which a divorce judgment is being attacked collaterally. Locate a case in your state in which a divorce judgment is being attacked directly (on appeal). Compare and contrast the procedures and issues involved in these two cases. Make a list of the similarities and a list of the differences between the two cases.

2. Identify and list the local officials who assist in the enforcement of child support obligations in your county or state. Your list should contain the title or name of the office or official, address, and telephone number for each. (ex. Prosecuting Attorney's Office, Child Support Enforcement Unit, Court Trustee's Office, Social Security Title IV-D Unit)

3. Contact one of the offices you identified in Number 2, above. Obtain any available information regarding the procedures for enforcing an existing child support obligation through that office.

    Make a list of these procedures in the order that they occur. This list should be clear and concise so that any child support recipient would be able to comprehend it without further explanation.

4. Determine whether your state or county provides for wage withholding as a method of collecting child support. If so, determine whether the withholding is automatically required by the court whenever child support is awarded, or if it is used only when the obligor becomes delinquent in payment.

    If the latter is true, determine what steps the recipient must take in order to obtain an order of income withholding. Make a concise list of these steps in the order that they must occur.

5. Research your state's statutes and locate the "long-arm" statute. Under what circumstances will it be applicable in a divorce proceeding? Locate a case from your state in which the "long-arm" statute was used to obtain personal jurisdiction over a defendant in a divorce case. Identify the circumstances of the case which provided the authority necessary for the court to apply the "long-arm" statute against the defendant? (ex. fathered a child in the state, lived within the state with the plaintiff while married)

ANSWERS TO REVIEW QUESTIONS:

Multiple choice.

1. B
2. D
3. A
4. E
5. A
6. C
7. D
8. B
9. C
10. A

Fill in the blank.

1. uncontested
2. domicile
3. ex parte
4. direct
5. collateral
6. subject matter
7. complaint (or petition)
8. summons
9. pro se
10. venue
11. interrogatories
12. requests for production
13. URESA, UIFSA
14. Full Faith and Credit
15. QDRO

Short answer.

1. Personal jurisdiction is the court's authority to make an order which is binding on a particular defendant. In rem jurisdiction is the court's authority to make an order which affects a thing, such as a marriage relationship.

2.	Subject matter jurisdiction is the court's authority to hear and decide a particular type of case, such as a divorce or criminal case. Venue designates the specific court (or county) within a state that has the authority to hear a particular divorce (or other) case based on the domicile of the parties.

3.	an order which is made and effective while a case is still being litigated

4.	A "long-arm" statute allows a court to obtain personal jurisdiction over a defendant who is no longer a resident of the state, but who had significant contacts with the state, such as having lived in the state while married to the plaintiff in a divorce proceeding.

5.	A guardian ad litem is an attorney who is appointed to represent the interests of a minor child during a particular civil proceeding, such as divorce.

6.	garnishment, writ of execution, QDRO

7.	A QMCSO requires a parent to maintain health insurance on a child when it is available through the parent's place of employment.

8.	interrogatories, requests for production, depositions

9.	when the parent seeking support lives in one state and the other parent from whom support is requested lives in another state. The action can proceed without requiring either parent to travel to another state.

10.	personal jurisdiction (also known as in personam jurisdiction)

Chapter 11

TAX CONSEQUENCES OF SEPARATION AND DIVORCE

REVIEW OF CHAPTER:
Tax consequences of divorce and separation agreements should be considered during negotiations. Alimony which qualifies under seven tests is deducted from income by the payor and reported as income by the recipient. Child support is not deducted or reported as income. Property division payments are not treated as taxable events. The transferee (recipient) of the property assumes the same basis the property had when it belonged to the transferor.

REVIEW QUESTIONS:

Multiple choice.
Select the correct answer from the choices provided.

1. In order to be able to deduct certain payments from his or her reported income, payor might negotiate an agreement which:

    a. characterizes certain payments as non-alimony
    b. characterizes certain payments as child support
    c. characterizes certain payments as alimony
    d. characterizes certain payment as property division
    e. both b and d

2. If payments to an ex-spouse are deducted by the payor, the result is:

    a. a reduction in the payor's adjusted gross income
    b. an increase in the payor's adjusted gross income
    c. a reduction in the recipient's adjusted gross income
    d. a reduction in alimony payments
    e. none of the above

3. In order for alimony payments to qualify as alimony:

a. the payment must be made in cash
b. the payment must be made under a divorce decree or separation agreement
c. the payment must be for the support of the minor children
d. the parties must file a joint tax return
e. both a and b ← *(circled)*

4. Significant changes in IRS rules impact on divorce decrees entered after:

   a. 1983
   b. 1984 ← *(circled)*
   c. 1985
   d. 1986
   e. 1990

5. If a payor is obligated under a divorce decree to make payments after the death of the recipient:

   a. the payments can be treated as alimony
   b. only the payments made before the death of the recipient can be treated as alimony
   c. only the payments made after the death of the recipient can be treated as alimony
   d. none of the payments can be treated as alimony ← *(circled)*

6. If a payment amount is to be reduced when a child dies or leaves home, the IRS will conclude that the payment is:

   a. alimony
   b. child support ← *(circled)*
   c. property division
   d. deductible by the payor
   e. income to the recipient

7. Under the "recapture rule", tax liability will be recalculated when parties have improperly:

   a. treated property division payments as alimony by front loading ← *(circled)*
   b. treated alimony as child support by making periodic payments
   c. treated child support as property division
   d. failed to report appreciation of property transferred under a divorce decree
   e. filed joint income tax returns

8. A property transfer is made "incident to divorce" under the new tax rules, if the transfer:

a. occurs within one year after the marriage ends
b. is related to the end of the marriage
c. occurs within six years after the marriage ends and is made under a divorce decree or separation agreement
d. all of the above ✓
e. none of the above

9. Fees paid to attorneys, accountants, and other professionals are deductible when the fee is paid in connection with:

   a. tax advice in connection with a divorce ✓
   b. obtaining child support
   c. obtaining alimony
   d. obtaining property
   e. a and c

10. When property is transferred incident to a divorce:

    a. the transferor does not deduct anything
    b. the transferee does not include anything in income
    c. the transferee must include the property as income
    d. the transferee retains the transferor's basis in the property
    e. a, b, and d ✓

Fill in the blank.
Fill in the blank with a term from Chapter 11.

1. A taxpayer's __AGI__ is total amount of income received, minus allowed deductions.

2. A _____ is an event that may or may not occur.

3. The effect of the __recapture__ rule is to require parties to recalculate tax liability when alimony has been improperly disguised as property division by front loading.

4. The person who transfers property to someone else is the __transferor__.

5. __appreciation__ is the increase in value of an item of property.

Chapter 11　　　STUDY GUIDE　　　83

6. An owner's _____ in property is the amount of the initial capital investment.

7. If certain tests are met, alimony payments are _____ to the payor and _____ to the recipient.

8. Under a _____ tax system, all taxpayers do not pay the same rate.

9. One test which must be met in order for alimony payments to qualify as alimony under the tax rules, is that the payments must be made in ___Cash___.

10. Parties who do not wish to treat certain payments as alimony may agree to treat these payments as ___non-alimony___.

11. Trying to disguise alimony as property division by making substantial "alimony" payments shortly after the separation or divorce is known as ___Front loading___.

12. A decrease in value of property is known as ___depreciation___.

13. A person to whom property is transferred is a ___transferee___.

14. ___Market value___ is the price that could be obtained in an open market between a willing buyer and a willing seller.

15. New tax rules governing a property division apply to property transfers that are _____ to a divorce.

Short answer.
Answer each of the following questions in one or two sentences.

1. What is the purpose of the "recapture rule"?

2. Under what circumstances will payments be presumed to be child support rather than alimony?

3. What is the primary distinction in the taxability of child support and alimony payments?

4. When is taxable gain realized in a situation requiring a spouse to transfer property to the other spouse as part of a divorce settlement?

5. What is meant by "adjusted basis" in property?

6. Why should tax consequences of payments be carefully considered during negotiations incident to divorce?

7. What portion of an attorney fee payment related to divorce could be deductible from taxpayer income?

8. Under the new tax rules which apply to payments made after 1984, when does a payment qualify as alimony?

9. What is the formula for determining the amount of taxable gain realized by a seller of property?

10. What is meant by "fair market value"?

PRACTICE EXERCISES:

1. Contact the IRS for available information or locate the portion of the United States Statutes that contains the Internal Revenue Code, and find the official definition of "income" as used by the IRS in determining federal income tax liability for wage earners. How does this definition apply to alimony, child support, and property division?

2. Consult the IRS or other sources for federal income tax forms (ex. your local public library, tax accountants, tax preparation services) and obtain a copy of the form which must be filed by custodial parents when the non-custodial parent will claim a minor child as a dependent.

ANSWERS TO REVIEW QUESTIONS:

Multiple choice.

1. C
2. A
3. E
4. B
5. D
6. B
7. A
8. D
9. E
10. E

Fill in the blank.

1. adjusted gross income
2. contingency
3. recapture
4. transferor
5. appreciation
6. basis
7. deductible, taxable
8. progressive
9. cash
10. nonalimony
11. front loading
12. depreciation
13. transferee
14. fair market value
15. incident

Short answer.

1. The recapture rule is designed to catch parties who have improperly attempted to disguise property division as alimony by making sizable payments soon after the marriage ends. The rule requires the payor to remove the deduction previously taken and include payments as income. The

recipient who previously included the alimony in income may now deduct it.

2. The IRS will presume that a payment is child support when the amount of the payment is to be reduced on the happening of a contingency relating to the child, or at a time that can be clearly associated with a contingency relating to the child.

3. Child support is not taxable as income to the recipient nor deductible from income of the payor. Alimony is taxable as income to the recipient and deductible from income of the payor.

4. Taxable gain is not realized at the time of transfer from one spouse to another, but is realized when the transferee sells the property.

5. Adjusted basis is the amount of the initial capital investment (basis), adjusted upward by the amount of capital improvements or downward.

6. Tax consequences can greatly impact the amount of income which each party will report on income tax returns. Deductibility or taxability will impact differently on individuals in different tax brackets. The real value of property, alimony, or child support should be considered in light of its taxability.

7. Only that portion of attorney fees incurred for tax advice and for acquiring alimony will be deductible.

8. A payment qualifies as alimony when it meets seven tests:
   1. made to a spouse or former spouse under divorce decree or separation agreement,
   2. parties do not file joint income tax return,
   3. parties are not members of same household when payment is made,
   4. payment is in cash,
   5. no obligation to make payments after recipient's death,
   6. payment is not treated as child support, and
   7. payment is not treated as "nonalimony".

9. (sale price) - (adjusted basis) = taxable gain

10. the price that could be obtained in an open market between a willing buyer and a willing seller dealing at arm's length

Chapter 12

THE LEGAL RIGHTS OF WOMEN

REVIEW OF CHAPTER:

States' Married Women's Property Acts changed common law to allow women to control their property in the same manner that men do. Federal laws require equal treatment for women in credit and employment. Title VII of the Civil Rights Act of 1964 prohibits discriminatory practices by employers. This Act has been interpreted to prohibit sexual harassment. Women's reproductive rights have been recognized under the Constitution by the U.S. Supreme Court in decisions such as Eisenstadt v. Baird and Roe v. Wade. Domestic violence remains a serious problem, although police departments and courts have begun to view these acts as crimes rather than "family matters" which were previously overlooked by the justice system.

REVIEW QUESTIONS:

Multiple choice.
Select the correct answer from the choices provided.

1. Married Women's Property Acts allowed:

    a. married women to retain their maiden names
    b. single women to own and control property
    c. married women to own and control property
    d. single women to vote
    e. married women to vote

2. Dower has been replaced in many states by:

    a. curtesy
    b. a forced share
    c. intestate distribution
    d. common law
    e. none of the above

Chapter 12   STUDY GUIDE   89

3. An example of an employer lawfully using a "BFOQ" in hiring is:

   a. hiring only male salespeople because customers prefer it
   b. hiring only female guards to "strip search" women prisoners
   c. hiring only male police officers because they are stronger
   d. hiring only female flight attendants because male passengers prefer it
   e. none of the above

4. Sexual harassment in employment is prohibited under:

   a. the equal protection clause of the U.S. Constitution
   b. Roe v. Wade
   c. the EEOC
   d. Title VII of the Civil Rights Act
   e. the Equal Pay Act

5. Complaints of discrimination in the workplace are investigated by a federal agency known as the:

   a. Fair Employment Practices Commission
   b. BFOQ
   c. Equal Pay Administration
   d. EEOC
   e. none of the above

6. The U.S. Supreme Court case which recognized the right of individuals to be free from governmental intrusion into decisions concerning contraception is:

   a. Roe v. Wade
   b. Planned Parenthood of Southeastern Pennsylvania v. Casey
   c. Buck v. Bell
   d. State v. Black
   e. Eisenstadt v. Baird

7. The U.S. Supreme Court case which recognized that a pregnant woman's right to privacy included the right to terminate her pregnancy (within certain state regulations) is:

   a. Roe v. Wade
   b. Planned Parenthood of Southeastern Pennsylvania v. Casey
   c. Buck v. Bell
   d. State v. Black

e. Eisenstadt v. Baird

8. The U.S. Supreme Court case which permitted states to require a pregnant woman's husband's consent before she has an abortion is:

a. Roe v. Wade
b. Planned Parenthood of Southeastern Pennsylvania v. Casey
c. Webster v. Reproductive Health Services
d. Eisenstadt v. Baird
e. none of the above, this would be a "substantial obstacle" to a woman's right to choose

9. A woman who seeks an injunction from the court ordering her husband to stop abusing her, usually obtains an order known as a:

a. restraining order
b. peace bond
c. protective order
d. both a and c are correct
e. none of the above

10. The battered wife syndrome has been used in some cases:

a. in which women have been prosecuted for murdering their husbands
b. in which men has been prosecuted for battering their wives
c. as a form of self-defense
d. but has never been successful
e. both a and c

Fill in the blank.
Fill in the blank with a term from Chapter 12.

1. Statutes which remove many legal disabilities imposed on married women regarding disposition of their property are known as _____.

2. At common law, _____ gave a widow lifetime use of one-third of her deceased husband's land which he owned during their marriage.

3. A person who dies _____ dies without leaving a valid will.

Chapter 12 — STUDY GUIDE

4. When used in relation to employment discrimination, BFOQ stands for _____.

5. In employment, unwelcome sexual advances to which an employee must submit in order to avoid being fired constitutes _____ under Title VII.

6. The federal agency known as the _____ has primary responsibility of enforcing Title VII of the Civil Rights Act.

7. _____ is the stage of fetal development at which an unborn child could survive outside the womb.

8. The decision of the U.S. Supreme Court in Roe v. Wade permitted states to regulate abortion procedures during the second and third _____ of a woman's pregnancy.

9. The decision of the U.S. Supreme Court in Planned Parenthood of Southeastern Pennsylvania v. Casey upheld the Roe decision, but stated that (even before fetal viability) states may pass laws which discourage abortion as long as the laws do not present _____ on a woman's right to seek an abortion.

10. An _____ is a court order requiring a person to do or to refrain from doing a particular thing, such as having contact with a spouse who has been the victim of abuse.

11. The term which is often used to describe a particular form of self-defense which may be raised by a woman charged with killing her abuse husband is the _____.

12. The right of a husband to the lifetime use of land his deceased wife owned during marriage is known as _____ under common law.

13. Under many states' present laws, the share of a deceased spouse's estate that a surviving spouse may elect to receive instead of what was provided under the deceased spouse's will is called a _____.

14. Under current laws, women are entitled to be treated the same way men are treated in matters involving _____ and _____.

15. The basis for a court invalidating a state law that unreasonably discriminates against women is found in the _____ Clause of the U.S. Constitution.

Short answer.
Answer each of the following questions in one or two sentences.

1. What is the primary role of the Equal Employment Opportunity Commission?

2. Name three things a woman may lawfully do today that women could not lawfully do under common law.

3. At common law, married women and unmarried women were treated differently. Name two things an unmarried woman could do that a married woman could not do at common law.

4. What legal steps must a woman take when she marries and wishes to retain her maiden name?

5. What legal steps must a woman take when she marries and wishes to assume her husband's last name?

6. What legal steps must a person take in order to change his or her name independent or marriage or divorce?

7. What damages may be obtained by a successful plaintiff who has been discriminated against by a creditor in violation of federal law?

8. What type of discrimination is prohibited by Title VII of the Civil Rights Act?

9. Under what circumstances may a BFOQ justify an employer's actions which result in different treatment for men and women?

10. What is meant by "sexual harassment"?

PRACTICE EXERCISES:

1. Locate any state statutes which exist in your state concerning abortion. Make a list of any restrictions on availability of abortion (ex. waiting period) or regulations (ex. in what facilities abortions may or may not be performed) currently in effect in your state.

2. Shepardize the statutes you listed in #1 or use the digests which index cases decided by the highest appellate court in your state, and look up the word "abortion." Have any cases been decided which specifically refer to any of the statutes you listed in #1, above? If so, select one of the cases and prepare a summary (brief) of the case.

3. Refer to your state statutes and determine if your state has passed a "Married Women's Property Act." If so, what was the effective date of this statute?

4. Does your city or state have a local agency which investigates claims of employment discrimination? If so, locate the complete name, address, and telephone number of the agency.

5. Contact a local bank, credit union, or other lending institution and obtain an application for a loan (ex. automobile loan, home loan, personal loan). Review the application and determine whether any information is requested which would identify the applicants' gender, age, marital status, or race. What laws are you aware of that would prevent a lender from using this information in deciding whether to approve an applicant's loan request?

ANSWERS TO REVIEW QUESTIONS:

Multiple choice.

1. C
2. B
3. B
4. D
5. D
6. E
7. A
8. E
9. D
10. E

Fill in the blank.

1. Married Women's Property Acts
2. dower
3. intestate
4. Bona Fide Occupational Qualification
5. sexual harassment
6. Equal Employment Opportunity Commission
7. viability
8. trimester
9. undue burdens (or substantial obstacle)
10. injunction
11. battered woman syndrome
12. curtesy
13. forced share
14. credit, employment
15. Equal Protection

Short answer.

1. to enforce Title VII of the Civil Rights Act, which prohibits employment discrimination based on race and sex

2. vote, make contracts, transfer property, serve on a jury, file a lawsuit

3. make contracts, transfer property

4. none

5. none

6. file a petition to change name in the appropriate state court, stating the reasons for the change; pay a fee to the court; publish a notice of the court proceeding in a local newspaper

7. punitive damages, court costs, and reasonable attorney's fees

8. discrimination with regard to hiring, discharge, compensation, terms, condition, or privileges of employment because of an individual's ... sex (also race or national origin)

9. if the BFOQ is reasonably necessary to the operation of a particular business or enterprise, not merely to accommodate the preferences of customers or co-workers

10. unwelcome sexual advances; requests for sexual favors; and other verbal or physical conduct of a sexual nature when it is a term or condition of employment; or is used as the basis for employment decisions; or unreasonably interferes with work performance or creates an intimidating, hostile, or offensive work environment

Chapter 13

ILLEGITIMACY AND PATERNITY PROCEEDINGS

REVIEW OF CHAPTER:

Under common law, children who were born out of wedlock could not inherit from either parent who died intestate, and fathers of illegitimate children had no duty to support. Today illegitimate children are treated the same as legitimate children regarding inheritance and support from their parents. Court proceedings are sometimes necessary to establish paternity. State statutes provide rebuttable presumptions concerning parentage. Blood and DNA testing provide scientific evidence which can be introduced in a paternity proceeding. Once paternity has been established, an order of support will also be made.

REVIEW QUESTIONS:

Multiple choice.
Select the correct answer from the choices provided.

1. Under common law, illegitimate children were:

    a. able to inherit from their mothers
    b. able to inherit from their fathers
    c. unable to inherit from either parent
    d. treated the same as legitimate children
    e. both a and b

2. Under states' laws today, illegitimate children are:

    a. not entitled to support from their fathers
    b. not entitled to support from their mothers
    c. unable to inherit from either parent
    d. entitled to support from both parents
    e. both a and b

Chapter 13 STUDY GUIDE 97

3. Various methods by which illegitimate children can be legitimated include all except:

   a. public acknowledgment by the father
   b. legitimation proceeding
   c. annulment
   d. paternity proceedings
   e. marriage between the parents

4. Federal law requires hospitals to:

   a. provide a form to be used by unmarried fathers to acknowledge paternity of newborn children
   b. conduct DNA tests on parents of all newborn children
   c. determine paternity of newborn children
   d. keep a fingerprint record of all unmarried fathers
   e. none of the above

5. In paternity proceedings, in order for the finding to be res judicata in any later proceeding filed by the child:

   a. the court's decision must be based on DNA evidence
   b. the court must have personal jurisdiction over the child
   c. the court must enter an order of child support
   d. the father must have signed an acknowledgement of paternity
   e. the child must have been a party to the earlier proceeding

6. Serology and genetic testing are often used as evidence in paternity proceedings. Of the available tests which measure the probability of paternity, the test which yields significantly accurate information as to whether a particular man is the father of a child (not merely an exclusion) is:

   a. ABO
   b. DNA
   c. Rh
   d. MNS
   e. blood grouping

7. If an indigent father is faced with defending a paternity action requiring genetic testing, and the father is unable to pay for the tests:

   a. the court will construe the lack of scientific evidence to require a finding of paternity against

the defendant
b. the state will be required to pay for the tests
c. the court will dismiss the case for lack of evidence
d. the court will require the testing lab to conduct the tests free of charge
e. none of the above

8. Under Lord Mansfield's rule, in paternity actions:

a. evidence that a married couple had not had sexual intercourse during the time the child was conceived could not be introduced
b. evidence that an unmarried couple had not had sexual intercourse during the time the child was conceived could not be introduced
c. evidence of sexual intercourse could not be introduced
d. blood tests could not be introduced as evidence
e. witnesses were not allowed to testify

9. The discovery of human blood groups and types has been of great assistance in paternity cases for all of the following reasons except:

a. blood types can be determined shortly after birth
b. blood types remain constant throughout an individual's life
c. blood types are inherited
d. no two people have the exact same blood type
e. blood samples are easily drawn

10. In most states, when a child is born through artificial insemination with the semen of a man other than the husband, and the husband consented to the insemination:

a. the husband has a duty to support the child
b. the semen donor has a duty to support the child
c. the child is considered legitimate
d. the child is considered illegitimate
e. both a and c

Fill in the blank.
Fill in the blank with a term from Chapter 13.

1. A scientific process used in paternity and criminal cases, in which the characteristics of an

Chapter 13 STUDY GUIDE 99

individual's molecular structure is viewed as a pattern of bands, is _____ testing.

2. The process of impregnation by a method other than sexual intercourse, such as by using the semen of a third-party donor, is the process of _____.

3. A _____ is a person appointed by the court to represent the interests of another (usually a minor).

4. A judgment is considered _____ when it was rendered "on the merits", thereby preventing the parties from relitigating the same dispute.

5. Statutes often refer to a man who is alleged or reputed to be a child's father as the _____ father.

6. A law that gives a state court personal jurisdiction over a nonresident based on his or her purposeful contact with the state is a _____ statute.

7. Blood grouping tests may be used to indicate the likelihood that a man is the father of a child. Although the tests cannot prove paternity with absolute certainty, they indicate the _____ of paternity.

8. In some states, a man who wishes to publicly acknowledge paternity of an out of wedlock child may record his acknowledgment in the state's_____.

9. A court proceeding in which the identify of a child's father is to be determined is a _____ proceeding.

10. At common law an _____ child could not inherit from either parent who died intestate.

11. A child whose parent dies due to the wrongful act of another, can bring a _____ action against defendants who caused the parent's death.

12. Although most laws today treat legitimate and illegitimate children equally, _____ laws impose stricter procedural burdens on illegitimate children claiming benefits.

13. A child born to a married woman is _____ to be legitimate unless conclusively proven otherwise.

14. Most paternity proceedings are filed by the states in an effort to determine paternity and to obtain an order of _____ for the benefit of the child.

15. In order for a court to enter a binding order of child support, the court must have _____ over the defendant/father.

Short answer.
Answer each of the following questions in one or two sentences.

1. At common law, in what ways were illegitimate children discriminated against?

2. In addition to determining whether a man is the father of a child, what is the main function of a paternity proceeding?

3. Why are many paternity proceedings filed by the state?

4. What is the significance of a judgment which is "res judicata"?

5. What actions might an unmarried father take to attempt to acknowledge his paternity of a child?

6. Explain why traditional blood group testing cannot establish the paternity of a particular defendant.

7. Briefly explain the significance of DNA testing in paternity proceedings.

8. Under Lord Mansfield's Rule what type of evidence could not be introduced in paternity actions?

9. Briefly identify three types of artificial insemination procedures.

10. What is the purpose of maintaining a Putative Father Registry?

PRACTICE EXERCISES:

1. Contact a local hospital and obtain a copy of the form provided for unmarried fathers to acknowledge paternity.

2. Consult your state statutes and code of state regulations to determine if a state-wide putative father registry is maintained in your state. If so, determine the steps a man must take to record his putative relationship to a child born out of wedlock.

3. Make a list of laboratories in your local area that are available to draw blood samples for use in paternity proceedings. Include the name, address, and telephone number of each laboratory you identify.

4. Research your state's probate code (statutes and case law, if necessary) and determine whether illegitimate children are entitled to inherit from their parents who leave property to their "children" in a will.

ANSWERS TO REVIEW QUESTIONS:

Multiple choice.

1. C
2. D
3. C
4. A
5. E
6. B
7. B
8. A
9. D
10. E

Fill in the blank.

1. DNA
2. artificial insemination
3. guardian ad litem
4. res judicata
5. putative
6. long arm
7. probability
8. putative father registry
9. paternity
10. illegitimate
11. wrongful death
12. Social Security
13. presumed
14. support
15. personal jurisdiction

Short answer.

1. Illegitimate children were not entitled to support from their fathers, nor could they inherit property from their parents who died intestate

2. to obtain an order of child support

3. to obtain an order of child support in situations where the mother is receiving ADC benefits

4. The judgment is a final determination of all issues which were litigated by the parties. No future action may be raised on these issues by any party to the former proceeding.

5. declare his paternity in a written registry of putative fathers maintained by the state, treat the child as his own, obtain a determination of paternity in a court proceeding

6. Blood types are not unique. Many individuals have the same blood types. Therefore a large number of men and women would have the blood types which could combine to form the blood type of any particular child. Traditional blood type grouping can only determine those individuals who could not have parented a particular child.

7. DNA testing can determine with a high degree of probability whether a particular person is the parent of a child. These results are possible because DNA is different in virtually every individual, with the exception of identical twins.

8. evidence that a married couple did not engage in sexual intercourse or were inaccessible during a period of time in which a child was conceived

9. AIH - artificial insemination with the semen of the husband; AID - artificial insemination with the semen of a third-party donor; AIC or CIA - artificial insemination in which the semen of the husband is mixed with that of a third-party donor

10. to allow unmarried men a chance to acknowledge their paternity, thus obligating themselves in future child support actions and making it possible to identify them in the event that other court proceedings arise (such as adoption of the child)

Chapter 14

THE LEGAL STATUS OF CHILDREN

REVIEW OF CHAPTER:
Minors are unemancipated individuals below the age of majority. Although 18 is the age of majority, some laws impose different age requirements for certain activities. Minors may disaffirm contracts and are processed as juvenile offenders or persons in need of supervision rather than as defendants in criminal proceedings. State agencies attempt to protect minors from abuse and neglect when necessary.

REVIEW QUESTIONS:

Multiple choice.
Select the correct answer from the choices provided.

1. The age of majority in most states is:

   a. 16
   b. 18
   c. 21
   d. none of the above

2. As a general rule, a minor:

   a. does not have legal capacity to enter a binding contract
   b. may disaffirm a contract before reaching majority
   c. may not own real estate
   d. may enter into binding contracts for automobiles
   e. both a and b

3. A minor who is involved in litigation will often be represented in court by:

   a. a legal guardian
   b. a parent

c. an attorney
d. a guardian ad litem
e. himself or herself

4. Although minors may generally disaffirm contracts, some states limit a minor's right to disaffirm certain types of contracts, such as:

   a. real estate contracts
   b. contracts for necessaries
   c. contracts between two minors
   d. contracts between a minor and an adult
   e. contracts for the purchase of an automobile

5. The domicile of a minor is:

   a. the domicile of the minor's mother
   b. the domicile of the minor's father
   c. the domicile of the minor's parents
   d. the state in which the minor chooses to live
   e. none of the above

6. If a court finds that a child has been neglected or abused by a parent, the court may:

   a. impose criminal penalties against the parent
   b. terminate the parent's parental rights
   c. place the child in the custody of the state
   d. all of the above
   e. a and c only

7. Examples of juvenile status offenses include:

   a. habitual truancy from school
   b. homicide
   c. aggravated assault
   d. incorrigibility at home
   e. both a and d

8. When a juvenile commits a serious act such as homicide or sexual assault:

   a. a judge may decide whether the juvenile will be tried as an adult
   b. the juvenile will be presumed to be incapable of having the necessary criminal intent to be

c. the juvenile will be placed in a foster home
   d. all of the above
   e. none of the above

9. A minor who is the subject of a juvenile court proceeding may be referred to as:

   a. a juvenile delinquent
   b. a PINS (Person In Need of Supervision)
   c. a MINS (Minor In Need of Supervision)
   d. a CHIPS (Child In Need of Protection and Services)
   e. all of the above

10. Children may be emancipated before the age of majority if an event occurs such as:

    a. the child joins the military
    b. the child's parents divorce
    c. the child enters into a contract
    d. the child commits a criminal act and is tried as an adult
    e. the child appears on the Oprah Winfrey Show

Fill in the blank.
Fill in the blank with a term from Chapter 14.

1. A person under the age of majority is a _____.

2. A loss of parental control over a child occurs when the child becomes legally independent, or is _____.

3. A minor has no legal obligation to perform a contract if he or she _____ the contract before reaching majority.

4. Items such as clothing, food, and shelter, which are needed to maintain a standard of living are referred to as _____, and minors may be unable to disaffirm contracts to purchase these items.

5. A _____ is a special person appointed by the court to represent the interests of another person.

6. The state where an adult has been physically present with the intent to make that place a permanent home is the person's _____.

7. Another word for "physical" punishment or discipline by a parent or teacher is _____ punishment.

8. _____ is the failure to provide support, medical care, education, moral example, or discipline necessary for a child's welfare.

9. A teacher who stands _____ has the authority to exercise some of the rights of a child's parents.

10. A young person under a designated age whose conduct would constitute a crime if committed by an adult is frequently called a _____.

Short answer.
Answer each of the following questions in one or two sentences.

1. Why were children considered incapable of committing crimes at common law?

2. What reason can you give for allowing minors to disaffirm contracts?

3. Give three examples of "necessaries."

4. What options does a court have in a situation of parental neglect of a child?

5. Under what circumstances might a child under age 18 be emancipated?

PRACTICE EXERCISES:

1. Consult the statutes of your state and locate the portion which applies to juvenile "crime." What terms are used to describe the individuals who are accused of the "criminal" acts? (ex. juvenile delinquents, juvenile offenders, PINS, etc.)

2. Consult the statutes of your state and locate the portion which applies to child abuse and neglect. What is the statutory definition of "abuse" and "neglect" in your state?

3. Consult the statutes of your state and determine the age of majority for most purposes (ex. making a contract or a will, and being emancipated from parental control). Now determine the age at which an individual may vote, obtain a marriage license without parental consent, and discontinue attending school.

Chapter 14 STUDY GUIDE 109

ANSWERS TO REVIEW QUESTIONS:

Multiple choice.

1. B
2. E
3. D
4. B
5. C
6. D
7. E
8. A
9. E
10. A

Fill in the blank.

1. minor
2. emancipated
3. disaffirms
4. necessaries
5. guardian ad litem
6. domicile
7. corporal
8. neglect
9. in loco parentis
10. juvenile delinquent

Short answer.

1. They were considered incapable of forming the required criminal intent because of their immaturity.

2. Minors are considered to be immature and innocent in some ways, and this provides them some protection from making unwise agreements or from being taken advantage of in an agreement.

3. food, clothing, medical treatment, shelter

4. termination of parental rights, criminal sanctions, placing the child in the custody of the state (foster care)

5. the child is living independently of the parents as a result of the child being married, joining the military, or obtaining a judgment of emancipation through a court proceeding

Chapter 15

ADOPTION

REVIEW OF CHAPTER:
Adoptions may be classified as agency adoptions or independent adoptions. Step-parent adoptions are considered independent adoptions. Black market adoptions are illegal. Before an adoption can occur, the natural parent's parental rights must be terminated. This termination may be voluntary (when the parent relinquishes his or her parental rights and consents to the adoption) or involuntary (when a court finds the parent to be unfit). Due process rights require that natural parents (married or unmarried) whose rights have not been terminated receive notice of the adoption. Adopted children receive all the rights and benefits of a natural child of the adoptive parents.

REVIEW QUESTIONS:

Multiple choice.
Select the correct answer from the choices provided.

1. The type of adoption which is illegal is:

    a. private adoption
    b. agency adoption
    c. black-market adoption
    d. interracial adoption
    e. step-parent adoption

2. One significant difference between agency adoptions and independent adoptions is that:

    a. independent adoptions do not involve court proceedings
    b. independent adoptions do not involve home studies of the adoptive parents
    c. independent adoptions do not require the termination of parental rights
    d. independent adoptions often involve private placement of a child by a relative, attorney, or physician
    e. none of the above

3. One action already taken by some states to attempt to reduce "black-market" adoptions is to:

   a. require an accounting for all payments and expenses connected with adoption
   b. eliminate independent adoptions
   c. recognize equitable adoptions
   d. prevent interracial adoptions
   e. disallow "open" adoptions

4. The natural parents' consent to adoption of their child is required unless:

   a. the natural parents are not married to each other
   b. the natural parents have been found to be unfit
   c. the child is old enough to consent to the adoption
   d. the adoptive parents do not wish to notify the natural parents
   e. both a and d

5. The Multiethnic Placement Act, passed by Congress in 1994 prohibits states from:

   a. allowing black-market adoptions
   b. allowing equitable adoptions
   c. delaying agency child placements
   d. allowing interracial child placements
   e. delaying child placements solely on the basis of race, color, or national origin

6. Some states have attempted to assure that a natural mother's voluntary relinquishment and consent to adoption of her child is valid by:

   a. requiring that she report all money paid to her for her child
   b. requiring that she sign the consent prior to the birth of her child
   c. requiring that she not sign the consent until at least 72 hours after the birth of her child
   d. allowing her a period of time in which she may revoke the consent
   e. both c and d

7. Some states permit the court to find that a natural parent's consent to adoption of his or her child is not required if:

   a. the parent has abandoned the child
   b. the parent has wilfully neglected the child
   c. the child is being adopted by a step-parent (married to the natural parent)
   d. both a and b
   e. none of the above

Chapter 15　　　　　　　　　　STUDY GUIDE　　　　　　　　　　113

8. What was the legal impact of the Florida Court of Appeals decision in <u>Kingsley v. Kingsley</u>?

   a. children could divorce their parents
   b. children in Florida can petition the court to terminate their parental rights
   c. children have standing to sue their parents
   d. both a and b
   e. none of the above

9. What primary legal principle did the Supreme Court of Illinois follow in <u>In re Doe & Doe</u>, the case which involved the attempted adoption of "Baby Richard"?

   a. the best interests of the child
   b. natural parents' right to receive due process notice before parental rights are terminated
   c. unwed fathers' rights to contest adoptions
   d. trial court judges misunderstand adoption law
   e. journalistic terrorism

10. Wrongful adoption is a tort in which adoptive parents seek damages from an agency for:

    a. removing a child from its adoptive parents' home
    b. requiring payment of an unreasonable fee from the adoptive parents
    c. failing to disclose available facts on the child's health
    d. delaying the placement of a child solely because of race
    e. both b and c

Fill in the blank.
Fill in the blank with a term from Chapter 15.

1. A child welfare service that provides shelter and temporary family care is referred to as _____ care.

2. A person who married the natural parent of a child, but who is not one of the child's natural parents is a _____.

3. In most states, after an adoption takes place, the adopted child's _____ will be reissued.

4. Baby buying is another term for _____ adoption.

5. The persons seeking to become the adoptive parents in an adoption proceeding are referred to as the _____.

6. In order for a court to have the power to hear an adoption matter, the court must have venue and _____ jurisdiction over the kind of case.

7. Due process of law requires that both natural parents be given _____ of the petition to adopt their child.

8. If a natural parent is found to be _____, the court may terminate his or her parental rights.

9. A natural parent who is willing to allow his or her child to be adopted will sign a written _____ permitting the court to proceed with the adoption.

10. In the case of "Gregory K", the primary legal issue for the court was whether a minor has _____ to file a suit on his own behalf.

11. In most states, after an adoption is final, the records are _____, making them unavailable.

12. In an _____ adoption, the natural parent maintains some contact with his or her child after the adoption.

13. In an _____ adoption, the child is considered the adopted child of a person who contracted to adopt, but failed to go through the formal adoption procedures.

14. In a _____ adoption, the adoptive parents seek damages from an agency which failed to disclose available information about the child's health or emotional condition.

15. Before a child becomes available for adoption, the _____ of both natural parents must be terminated.

Short answer.
Answer each of the following questions in one or two sentences.

Chapter 15 — STUDY GUIDE — 115

1. Why do some states require adoptive parents to report all payments made in connection with adoption of a child?

2. Under what circumstances might adoptive parents bring a tort action for "wrongful adoption"?

3. What is the usual role of foster care in adoption proceedings?

4. Under what general circumstances will a court find that a natural parent's consent to adoption is not required?

5. What action by a natural parent might be the basis for a court to find that he or she is "unfit"?

6. What is the legal relationship between an adopted child and his or her adoptive parents once the adoption is final?

7. On what legal principle did the Florida Court of Appeals overturn the trial court decision in the "Gregory K" case?

8. Under what conditions might a natural parent be allowed to revoke his or her consent to adoption of a child?

9. Under what conditions might an "equitable adoption" be recognized?

10. What is meant by an "open adoption"?

PRACTICE EXERCISES:

1. Consult your state statutes to determine what efforts have been made by the legislature to discourage black market adoptions. (ex. statutes might prohibit adoption advertising by private individuals or require a report of all money paid).

2. Contact a local child placement agency (public or private) and determine what restrictions (if any) they have on who may adopt. (ex. single individuals, members of a race other than the race of the child, only members of a particular religious faith).

3. Determine who (agency or court appointed social service worker) is responsible for conducting petitioners' home studies prior to adoptions in your local area. Contact a representative or social worker and make a list of factors they consider and evaluate in the petitioners' home prior to making a recommendation to the court.

Chapter 15　　　　　　　　　　STUDY GUIDE

ANSWERS TO REVIEW QUESTIONS:

Multiple choice.

1. C
2. D
3. A
4. B
5. E
6. E
7. D
8. E
9. B
10. C

Fill in the blank.

1. foster
2. stepparent
3. birth certificate
4. black market
5. petitioners
6. subject matter
7. notice
8. unfit
9. consent
10. standing
11. sealed
12. open
13. equitable
14. wrongful
15. parental rights

Short answer.

1. to avoid baby buying

2. if an agency had failed to tell the adoptive parents about the child's background, health, or

emotional history, and the parents would not have wanted to adopt the child if they had known the truth

3. to provide a temporary home placement for a child who is unable to reside with his or her natural parents

4. if the parent has already voluntarily consented to relinquish the child for adoption, or if the parent is found to be unfit due to abandonment or neglect of the child

5. extreme cruelty or abuse, neglect, or abandonment of the child

6. the child has the same legal relationship as a natural child of the parents, including the right to inherit, support, and use of the parents' surname

7. an unemancipated minor does not have standing to sue on his own behalf

8. if the consent was given involuntarily as a result of duress or coercion

9. if the adult had agreed and intended to adopt a child, but had not completed the required legal proceedings

10. the natural parent maintains some degree of contact with the adopted child and his or her adoptive parents

Chapter 16

SURROGACY AND THE NEW SCIENCE OF MOTHERHOOD

REVIEW OF CHAPTER:

Surrogate motherhood may be achieved through artificial insemination and in vitro fertilization. State legislatures have responded to the legal issues raised by this new medical technology in various ways. Some have passed no legislation regulating surrogacy; others have prohibited surrogacy contracts altogether, and some have established specific regulations to be applied to surrogacy agreements. The "Uniform Status of Children of Assisted Conception Act" is a model act proposed by the National Conference of Commissioners on Uniform State Laws, and is available for consideration by individual states.

REVIEW QUESTIONS:

Multiple choice.
Select the correct answer from the choices provided.

1. The four general methods of surrogate parenting include all of the following except:

    a. sexual intercourse
    b. artificial insemination by husband
    c. in-vitro fertilization
    d. artificial insemination by donor
    e. natural insemination

2. The most common method of surrogate parenting is:

    a. sexual intercourse
    b. artificial insemination by husband
    c. in-vitro fertilization
    d. artificial insemination by donor
    e. natural insemination

3. The primary reason couples seek surrogate mothers stems from:

   a. lack of children available for adoption
   b. courts' willingness to enforce surrogate contracts
   c. female infertility
   d. male infertility
   e. public policy

4. A major concern in state legislatures with regard to surrogacy contracts is:

   a. capacity to contract
   b. best interests of the child
   c. involuntary servitude
   d. fee agreements
   e. exploitation of women

5. Opponents to surrogacy argue all of the following except:

   a. the courts will be overwhelmed with surrogacy contract disputes
   b. children born to surrogates will be psychologically damaged
   c. surrogacy will result in economic exploitation of rich over poor people
   d. there are many children available for adoption

6. Advocates of surrogacy argue that:

   a. surrogacy contracts will reduce the number of abortions
   b. a decreasing number of babies available for adoption means that more couples will seek out surrogate mothers
   c. a limit on fees and regulation of brokers will ensure competency, honesty and legitimacy
   d. surrogacy is a way to avoid interracial adoption
   e. both b and c

7. Adoption laws in most states may indirectly impact on surrogacy contracts because:

   a. adoption laws prohibit a mother from consenting to adoption before the child is born
   b. adoption laws prohibit artificial insemination
   c. adoption laws forbid payment of compensation in exchange for the mother's consent to an adoption
   d. none of the above
   e. both a and c

Chapter 16 — STUDY GUIDE

8. If terms of surrogate contracts are breached by either party, courts may be faced with enforcement issues such as:

   a. neither the surrogate nor the intended parents want a child who is born with a disability
   b. the surrogate decides to keep the baby
   c. the intended parents refuse to pay the surrogate's fee
   d. the surrogate chooses to have an abortion during the first trimester of pregnancy
   e. all of the above

9. The primary difference between a commercial surrogacy contract and a noncommercial surrogacy contract is that:

   a. in a commercial contract, a broker is involved as an intermediary
   b. in a noncommercial contract, the parties are related to each other
   c. in a commercial contract, a payment is made to the surrogate to cover fees and expenses
   d. in a noncommercial contract, there is no court decision to establish parentage

Fill in the blank.
Fill in the blank with a term from Chapter 16.

1. The most common form of surrogate parenting is _____ by _____.

2. The method of surrogacy in which a sperm and an egg are joined in a laboratory and the fertilized egg is implanted in the surrogate is _____ fertilization.

3. The person who charges a fee for facilitating the surrogacy arrangement by bringing the surrogate and couple together is an _____.

4. A _____ is an organism produced by the union of two gametes.

5. A _____ is a cell that participates in fertilization and development of a new organism, and is also known as a germ cell or sex cell.

6. A woman who enters a contract to become pregnant, to give birth to a child, and then to relinquish all parental rights to someone else upon birth of the child is a _____.

7. Couples who enter contracts with women who will give birth and then relinquish all parental rights to the couple are the _____.

8. A uniform law which addresses surrogacy contracts refers to the children born from these agreements as "children of _____."

9. A concern of those who seek to regulate surrogacy contracts is the fear that fees paid to surrogates may actually involve the prohibited act of _____.

10. A woman who provides an ovum or a man who provides sperm for the fertilization process in a surrogacy contract is called a _____.

Short answer.
Answer each of the following questions in one or two sentences.

1. Identify two arguments that can be made in support of surrogacy contracts.

2. Identify two arguments that can be made in opposition to surrogacy contracts.

3. Why have some states failed to pass any legislation regulating surrogacy contracts?

4. Identify two possible disputes that could arise between intended parents and a surrogate.

5. How might surrogacy contracts violate public policy?

6. Why do some couples prefer surrogacy over adoption?

Chapter 16 STUDY GUIDE

7. What is the role of an intermediary in a surrogacy arrangement?

8. What is the most common form of surrogacy?

PRACTICE EXERCISES:

1. Consult your state statutes and determine if there are any laws which allow, disallow, or regulate surrogacy contracts.

2. Contact a fertility clinic or reproductive health specialist in your area and obtain any available information concerning artificial insemination and other forms of surrogacy. You might be able to request information about procedures, costs, and contractual terms.

3. Try to locate the name and address of a surrogate intermediary (or broker). Find out what kind of screening they perform on surrogates and intended parents.

ANSWERS TO REVIEW QUESTIONS:

Multiple choice.

1. A
2. B
3. C
4. D
5. A
6. C
7. E
8. E
9. C

Fill in the blank.

1. artificial insemination by husband
2. in-vitro
3. intermediary
4. zygote
5. gamete
6. surrogate
7. intended parents
8. assisted conception
9. baby selling
10. donor

Short answer.

1. regulation of fees promotes honesty, competency and legitimacy; proper examination of couples and surrogates would ensure emotional and financial responsibility

2. it violates the Thirteenth Amendment; it promotes baby selling

3. State legislatures do not know what position to take with regard to surrogacy contracts and the rapidly changing medical technology.

4. The surrogate could refuse to give the child up for adoption after birth; the parents could

refuse to take the child if he or she is born with a disability.

5.   by exploiting the poor over the rich, or by constituting baby selling

6.   Surrogacy can provide a genetic link to one of the intended parents.

7.   The intermediary locates the surrogate and matches her with the couple.

8.   Artificial insemination by husband

Chapter 17

TORTS

REVIEW OF CHAPTER:

Torts are civil wrongs that cause harm to persons or property, for which courts will provide remedies. Intrafamily torts that damage property may be the basis of a lawsuit in all states. However, some states provide immunity from suit for personal injury torts committed by family members. In many states which provide intrafamily immunity for personal injury liability, it only applies to negligence torts, not to intentional torts.

Tort claims which may be filed against third parties include claims for loss of consortium of a spouse, wrongful-birth, and wrongful-pregnancy, along with several non-derivative tort claims such as alienation of affections, criminal conversation, enticement of a spouse, abduction of a child, and seduction. Most courts do not allow a child's action for wrongful life.

Under some limited circumstances a family member may be vicariously liable for the actions of another family member which results in a tort.

REVIEW QUESTIONS:

Multiple choice.
Select the correct answer from the choices provided.

1. Intentional torts against a person include all of the following EXCEPT:

    a. trespass
    b. assault
    c. battery
    d. libel
    e. false imprisonment

2. In states which retain some form of intrafamily tort immunity, the immunity generally applies to:

a. torts against property
b. intentional torts against an emancipated child
c. negligence against a person
d. torts against children
e. torts against a spouse's property

3. In states where intrafamily tort immunity exists, it usually applies to tort claims between:

   a. a parent and a child
   b. a husband and wife
   c. brothers and sisters
   d. grandparents and grandchildren
   e. both a and b

4. Intrafamily tort immunity does not:

   a. prevent tort claims between spouses
   b. prevent criminal prosecution for acts against family members
   c. prevent tort claims by emancipated children against parents
   d. prevent tort claims by children against parents
   e. both b and c

5. A tort action brought against a doctor by parents of an unwanted deformed or impaired child is an action for:

   a. wrongful life
   b. wrongful birth
   c. wrongful pregnancy
   d. wrongful death
   e. loss of consortium

6. In most states, a claim for loss of consortium may only be brought by:

   a. a married person for injuries to his or her spouse caused by a third person
   b. a married person for his or her own injuries caused by a third party
   c. a parent for injuries to his or her child
   d. any individual who is dependent on someone else for companionship

7. In most states, a claim for loss of services may only be brought by:

   a. a married person for injuries to his or her spouse caused by a third person

b. a married person for his or her own injuries caused by a third party
c. a parent for injuries to his or her child
d. any individual who is dependent on someone else for companionship
e. both a and b

8. Examples of a <u>nonderivative</u> tort action which may be brought by a family member because of what the defendant did to another family member include:

a. assault
b. loss of consortium
c. alienation of affections
d. wrongful birth
e. intentional infliction of emotional distress

9. Generally one family member is not liable for the torts of another family member. Exceptions to this rule include:

a. situations in which state statutes apply to make parents vicariously liable on a limited basis for their children's torts
b. situations in which the family purpose doctrine applies
c. situations in which the parent was negligent by failing to adequately control the child
d. situations in which an emancipated minor commits a tort
e. both a and b

Fill in the blank.
Fill in the blank with a term from Chapter 17.

1. _____ is unreasonable conduct that causes injury or damage to someone to whom a duty of reasonable care was owed by the defendant.

2. When a defendant is liable because of what someone else has done, that defendant is _____ liable.

3. Plaintiffs who hope to recover monetary damages will sue the defendant with _____, which means the defendant has sufficient resources to pay a judgment award.

4. A derivative claim which a parent may file against an individual who causes injury to the

Chapter 17 — STUDY GUIDE — 129

parent's child is a claim for _____.

5. A derivative claim which a spouse may file against an individual who causes injury to the other spouse is a claim for _____.

6. A tort claim which is dependent on an underlying wrongful act to someone else is a _____ claim.

7. An action by parents to recover their damages caused by the birth of an unwanted impaired child is a claim for _____.

8. Although intrafamily immunity may prevent tort claims between family members, states can always _____ one family member for crimes committed against another family member.

9. An intrafamily tort is a tort committed by _____ against _____.

10. _____ is a defense that prevents someone from being sued for what would otherwise be wrongful conduct.

11. A tort which is committed willfully or as a result of a voluntary act (rather than a careless breach of duty) is an _____ tort.

12. A tort which results from a defendant's wrongful entry onto the property of the plaintiff is _____.

13. A tort which results from a defendant's written statements that are false and that injure the plaintiff's reputation is _____.

14. A tort which results from a defendant's oral statements that are false and that injure the plaintiff's reputation is _____.

Short answer.
Answer each of the following questions in one or two sentences.

1. What is the impact of intrafamily tort immunity when applied to a defendant in a tort claim filed by his or her spouse?

2. Give two historical reasons for the recognition of intrafamily tort immunity.

3. Name two instances in which parents may be vicariously liable for torts committed by children.

4. Explain the term "vicarious liability" as it might be applied to an employer and employee.

5. How would the doctrine of intrafamily tort immunity affect a spouse's claim against the other spouse for damage to property?

6. How are emancipated and unemancipated children treated differently with regard to intrafamily tort immunity?

7. What is meant by a "derivative" tort claim?

8. Why have most states refused to recognize an impaired or deformed child's claim for wrongful life?

9. What direct claim for negligence may be filed against a parent whose child commits a tort?

10. Name three nonderivative actions which may be filed against someone who committed a tort by doing certain acts with or to another family member.

Chapter 17 STUDY GUIDE

PRACTICE EXERCISES:

1. Consult your state statutes and determine if a statute exists which creates limited vicarious liability for parents whose children commit torts.
   a) Does it apply to only intentional torts, or to both intentional torts and negligence?
   b) What is the amount of monetary damage which may be assessed against parents under this statute?

2. Consult the digest to decisions by courts in your state and look for cases which refer to intrafamily tort immunity. Read several cases and determine whether courts in your state recognize intrafamily tort immunity. If the doctrine of immunity is recognized, does it apply to negligence claims or intentional tort claims, or both?

3. Consult the digest to decisions by courts in your state and look for cases which involve claims for wrongful birth or wrongful life. How did the courts decide these cases?
   a) Is wrongful birth a recognized cause of action in your state? If so, who may bring such an action, and what must the plaintiff allege? What damages may be recovered?
   b) Is wrongful life a recognized cause of action in your state? If so, who may bring such an action, and what must the plaintiff allege? What damages may be recovered?

ANSWERS TO REVIEW QUESTIONS:

Multiple choice.

1. A
2. C
3. E
4. E
5. B
6. A
7. C
8. C
9. E

Fill in the blank.

1. negligence
2. vicariously
3. deep pockets
4. loss of services
5. loss of consortium
6. derivative
7. wrongful birth
8. criminally prosecute
9. one family member; another family member
10. immunity
11. intentional
12. trespass
13. libel
14. slander

Short answer.

1. It is a defense. It makes the defendant's acts non-tortious; therefore the defendant cannot be liable to the plaintiff.

2. It may have an adverse impact on family harmony, and it may tempt family members who are covered by insurance to commit conspiracy or to commit fraud.

3.   where state statutes provide for such liability on a limited basis, and where the family purpose doctrine is applied

4.   If an employee commits an act which causes injury (a tort), the employer may be held responsible (liable) for the employee's acts even though the employer committed no wrong.

5.   Intrafamily tort immunity does NOT apply to claims for property damage.

6.   Intrafamily tort immunity does NOT apply to claims by unemancipated children against their parents.

7.   There must be an underlying wrong (tort) committed against a family member before the other family member's derivative action may be allowed. The original tort is the basis for the derivative action.

8.   It would be difficult to measure the damages. No one could compare the value of the deformed child's present life against the value of not having been born.

9.   failure to adequately supervise or control the child's conduct

10. alienation of affections, criminal conversation, enticement, abduction of a child, seduction